INTRODUCTION

GW01048603

A comprehensive statistical review...

Following hard on the heels of a successful Itali; return of English clubs to European competition has sparked off an unprecedented level of interest in international football.

So it is a particular pleasure to present for the first time this handy new football booklet which aims to provide an immediate statistical review of the European season just completed.

Eurosoccer Statistics 1991 contains a wealth of statistics on the 1990/91 season, providing an accurate and detailed work of reference which should appeal to all followers of the European game.

All 35 UEFA nations are featured – final championship tables, top goalscorers, cup results and details of promoted and relegated teams cover the domestic scene.

National team and European Cups results, together with a list of all next season's European competition qualifiers, complete the international section.

All, in all, a concise and comprehensive statistical review of all the major events in European football over the past 12 months.

Published in Great Britain July 1991 by Sports Projects Ltd

188 Lightwoods Hill, Smethwick, Warley, West Midlands B67 5EH

Copyright © 1990 Sports Projects Ltd

ISBN 0 946866 02 3   Price £2.95

Produced & Designed by Bernard Gallagher

Statistics compiled by Mike Hammond

Cover photograph by Ross Kinnaird, Empics Ltd

Printed by Peerless Press Ltd, Spon Lane, West Bromwich B70 6AQ

ALBANIA

CHAMPIONSHIP TABLE 90-91

		Pd	W	D	L	F	A	Pt	GD
1	FLAMURTARI	39	24	6	9	63	32	54	+31
2	PARTIZANI	39	18	12	9	52	35	48	+17
3	VLLAZNIA	39	16	13	10	57	48	45	+9
4	17 NENTORI	39	16	12	11	52	40	44	+12
5	TOMORI	39	13	14	12	62	47	40	+15
6	DINAMO	39	13	14	12	53	44	40	+9
7	APOLONIA	39	13	12	14	49	47	38	+2
8	LOKOMOTIVA	39	12	12	15	31	38	36	-7
9	LABINOTI	39	11	14	14	29	37	36	-8
10	SKENDERBEU	39	10	15	14	46	55	35	-9
11	BESA	39	11	12	16	45	50	34	-5
12	KASTRIOTI	39	12	10	17	41	62	34	-21
13	TRAKTORI	39	10	12	17	39	60	32	-21
14	LUFTETARI	39	12	6	21	31	55	30	-24

Relegated - LUFTETARI
Promoted - 3 teams (undecided at press time)

DOMESTIC CUP 90-91

Quarters	Flamurtari v 17 Nentori	2-0	0-1	(agg. 2-1)
	Kastrioti v **Dinamo**	2-1	1-3	(agg. 3-4)
	Partizani v Besa	2-0	2-0	(agg. 4-0)
	Apolonia v Luftetari	2-0	0-0	(agg. 2-0)

Semis	**Partizani**	1	Apolonia	0
	Flamurtari	4	Dinamo	1

Final	Partizani	1	Flamurtari	1

(a.e.t. 4-3 on pens.)

TOP GOALSCORERS

29	Bozgo	(Tomori)
27	Raklli	(Besa)
16	Kepa	(Vllaznia)
14	Tahiri	(Dinamo)

EUROPEAN CUPS

Champions' Cup
DINAMO TIRANA
1st round   Marseille (France)
A 1-5, H 0-0, (agg. 1-5)

Cup-winners' Cup
FLAMURTARI VLORA
1st round   Olympiakos (Greece)
A 1-3, H 0-2, (agg. 1-5)

UEFA Cup
PARTIZANI TIRANA
1st round   Universitatea Craiova
(Romania)
H 0-1, A 0-1, (agg. 0-2)

1990/91 Qualifiers
Champions' Cup   Flamurtari Vlora
Cup-winners' Cup Partizani Tirana
UEFA Cup   Vllaznia Shkoder

NATIONAL TEAM RESULTS 90-91

05/09/90	Greece	A	Patras	0-1	
17/11/90	France (ECQ)	H	Tirana	0-1	
19/12/90	Spain (ECQ)	A	Seville	0-9	
30/03/91	France (ECQ)	A	Paris	0-5	
01/05/91	Czechoslovakia (ECQ)	H	Tirana	0-2	
26/05/91	Iceland (ECQ)	H	Tirana	1-0	Abazi

CHAMPIONSHIP TABLE 90-91

		Pd	W	D	L	F	A	Pt	GD
1	FK AUSTRIA	36	22	7	7	72	33	36	+39
2	FC TIROL	36	21	9	6	78	35	35	+43
3	STURM GRAZ	36	18	9	9	60	37	32	+23
4	RAPID VIENNA	36	18	5	13	67	41	27	+26
5	CASINO SALZBURG	36	15	7	14	58	48	24	+10
6	ADMIRA WACKER	36	9	14	13	31	48	23	-17
7	VORWARTS STEYR	36	10	12	14	46	57	21	-11
8	DSV ALPINE	36	9	11	16	38	61	19	-23
9	WIENER S-C	22	7	3	12	25	42	17	-17
10	FIRST VIENNA	22	6	5	11	29	48	17	-19
11	SC KREMS	22	3	7	12	18	40	13	-22
12	VSE ST. POLTEN	22	3	5	14	18	50	11	-32

N.B. After 22 matches the top eight play off for the title, taking half their points total. Half points are rounded upwards. The bottom four enter a promotion/relegation play-off group with the top four Second Division clubs.

Relegated – WIENER SPORT-CLUB
Promoted – VOEST LINZ

DOMESTIC CUP 90-91

Quarter-Finals	FC Salzburg 1	**Rapid Vienna 5**
	LUV Graz 2	Sturm Graz 1
	Wiener Sport-Club 1	Casino Salzburg 0
	Stockerau 3	VOEST Linz 1
Semi-Finals	**Stockerau 1**	Wiener Sport-Club 0
	LUV Graz 0	**Rapid Vienna 1**
Final	**Stockerau 2**	Rapid Vienna 1

NATIONAL TEAM 90/91

21/08/90	Switzerland	H	Vienna	1-3 Ogris A.
12/09/90	Faeroe Is. (ECQ)	A	Landskrona	0-1
31/10/90	Yugoslavia (ECQ)	A	Belgrade	1-4 Ogris A.
14/11/90	N. Ireland (ECQ)	H	Vienna	0-0
17/04/91	Norway	H	Vienna	0-0
01/05/91	Sweden	A	Solna	0-6
22/05/91	Faeroe Is. (ECQ)	H	Salzburg	3-0 Pfeifenberger, Streiter, Wetl
05/06/91	Denmark (ECQ)	A	Odense	1-2 Ogris E.

TOP GOALSCORERS

29	Danek	(FC Tirol)
23	Bierhoff	(Casino Salzburg)
16	Fjortoft	(Rapid Vienna)
14	Westerthaler	(FC Tirol)
13	Pacult	(FC Tirol)

EUROPEAN CUPS

Champions' Cup

FC TIROL
1st round   FC Kuusysi (Finland)
             H 5-0, A 2-1, (agg. 7-1)
2nd round   Real Madrid (Spain)
             A 1-9, H 2-2, (agg. 3-11)

Cup-winners' Cup

FK AUSTRIA
1st round   PSV Schwerin
             (East Germany)
             A 2-0, H 0-0, (agg. 2-0)
2nd round   Juventus (Italy)
             H 0-4, A 0-4, (agg. 0-8)

UEFA Cup

RAPID VIENNA
1st round   Internazionale (Italy)
             H 2-1, A 1-3, (agg. 3-4)

ADMIRA WACKER
1st round   Vejle (Denmark)
             A 1-0, H 3-0, (agg. 4-0)
2nd round   Luzern (Switzerland)
             A 1-0, H 1-1, (agg.2-1)
3rd round   Bologna (Italy)
             H 3-0, A 0-3, (agg. 3-3; 5-6 on pens.)

1991/92 Qualifiers

Champions' Cup	FK Austria
Cup-winners' Cup	Stockerau
UEFA Cup	FC Tirol
	Sturm Graz

CHAMPIONSHIP TABLE 90-91

		Pd	W	D	L	F	A	Pt	GD
1	ANDERLECHT	34	23	7	4	74	22	53	+52
2	MECHELEN	34	20	10	4	59	24	50	+35
3	GENT	34	20	7	7	67	37	47	+30
4	CLUB BRUGES	34	18	11	5	61	27	47	+34
5	GERMINAL EKEREN	34	17	8	9	55	41	42	+14
6	STANDARD LIEGE	34	16	10	8	51	42	42	+9
7	ANTWERP	34	11	14	9	54	45	36	+9
8	CHARLEROI	34	9	15	10	36	36	33	=
9	LOKEREN	34	12	8	14	41	45	32	-4
10	FC LIEGE	34	11	10	13	42	45	32	-3
11	LIERSE	34	9	11	14	26	41	29	-15
12	RWDM	34	10	8	16	40	45	28	-5
13	WAREGEM	34	8	12	14	33	45	28	-12
14	GENK	34	9	8	17	31	66	26	-35
15	KORTRIJK	34	10	5	19	41	57	25	-16
16	CERCLE BRUGES	34	9	7	18	40	73	25	-33
17	ST-TRUIDEN	34	6	10	18	30	51	22	-21
18	BEERSCHOT	34	5	5	24	33	72	15	-39

Relegated - ST-TRUIDEN, BEERSCHOT
Promoted - BEVEREN, EENDRACHT AALST

DOMESTIC CUP 90-91

Quarter-Finals
FC Liege v **Lokeren** 1-0 1-5 (agg. 2-5)
Charleroi v **Lommel** 0-2 1-3 (agg. 1-5)
Antwerp v **Mechelen** 0-1 0-1 (agg. 0-2)
Club Bruges v Beveren 1-0 1-1 (agg. 2-1)

Semi-Finals
Lokeren v **Mechelen** 1-3 1-1 (agg. 2-4)
Club Bruges v Lommel 1-0 1-0 (agg. 2-0)

Final
Club Bruges 3   Mechelen 1

NATIONAL TEAM 90-91

12/09/90	East Germany	H	Brussels	0-2	
17/10/90	Wales (ECQ)	A	Cardiff	1-3	Versavel
13/02/91	Italy	A	Terni	0-0	
27/02/91	L'bourg (ECQ)	H	Brussels	3-0	Vandenbergh, Ceulemans, Scifo
27/03/91	Wales (ECQ)	H	Brussels	1-1	Degryse
01/05/91	Germany (ECQ)	A	Hanover	0-1	

TOP GOALSCORERS

23	Vandenbergh	(Gent)
20	Weber	(Cercle Bruges)
19	Nilis	(Anderlecht)
18	Oliveira	(Anderlecht)
	Hofmans	(Germinal Ekeren)

EUROPEAN CUPS

Champions' Cup
CLUB BRUGES
1st round   Lillestrom (Norway)
            A 1-1, H 2-0, (agg. 3-1)
2nd round   Milan (Italy)
            A 0-0, H 0-1, (agg. 0-1)

Cup-winners' Cup
FC LIEGE
1st round   Viking (Norway)
            A 2-0, H 3-0, (agg. 5-0)
2nd round   Estrela Amadora (Portugal)
            H 2-0, A 0-1, (agg. 2-1)
Quarter   Juventus (Italy)
            H 1-3, A 0-3, (agg. 1-6)

UEFA Cup
ANDERLECHT
1st round   Petrolul Ploiesti (Romania)
            H 2-0, A 2-0, (agg. 4-0)
2nd round   Omonia Nicosia (Cyprus)
            A 1-1, H 3-0, (agg. 4-1)
3rd round   Borussia Dortmund (W Germany)
            H 1-0, A 1-2, (agg. 2-2)
            won on away goals
Quarter   Roma (Italy)
            A 0-3, H 2-3, (agg. 2-6)

MECHELEN
1st round   Sporting (Portugal)
            A 0-1, H 2-2, (agg. 2-3)
ANTWERP
1st round   Ferencvaros (Hungary)
            H 0-0, A 1-3, (agg. 1-3)

1991/92 Qualifiers
Champions' Cup   Anderlecht
Cup-winners' Cup   Club Bruges
UEFA Cup   Mechelen
                   Gent
                   Germinal Ekeren

CHAMPIONSHIP TABLE 90-91

		Pd	W	D	L	F	A	Pt	GD
1	ETAR TARNOVO	30	18	8	4	49	21	44	+28
2	CSKA SOFIA	30	14	9	7	51	28	37	+23
3	SLAVIA SOFIA	30	14	9	7	48	29	37	+19
4	LOK. SOFIA	30	13	10	7	50	36	36	+14
5	BOTEV PLOVDIV	30	13	10	7	49	41	36	+8
6	LEVSKI SOFIA	30	12	9	9	51	38	33	+13
7	CHERNOMORETS	30	11	8	11	41	50	30	-9
8	LOK. G.O.	30	13	3	14	42	39	29	+3
9	BEROE S. ZAGORA	30	10	7	13	38	41	27	-3
10	MINIOR PERNIK	30	10	7	13	36	44	27	-8
11	LOK. PLOVDIV	30	9	9	12	34	42	27	-8
12	PIRIN BLAG'VGRAD	30	11	4	15	38	40	26	-2
13	SLIVEN	30	9	8	13	39	49	26	-10
14	YANTRA GABROVO	30	9	8	13	31	44	26	-13
15	DUNAV RUSE	30	8	6	16	23	42	22	-19
16	KHASKOVO	30	7	3	20	27	63	17	-36

Relegated - DUNAV RUSE, KHASKOVO
Promoted - KHEBAR PAZARDSHIK, DOBRUDZHA DOBRICH

DOMESTIC CUP 90-91

Quarter-Final Group Standings
(A) 1. Botev P., 2. Chernomorets, 3. Pirin Blag., 4. Akademik.
(B) 1. Lok. Sofia, 2. Slavia, 3. Pirin G. Delchev, 4. Lok. Plovdiv.
(C) 1. Etar, 2. Beroe, 3. Yantra, 4. Spartak Varna.
(D) 1. Levski, 2. CSKA, 3. Khebar Paz., 4. Chumerna Elena.

Semis   Lok. Sofia v **Levski Sofia**   2-3 1-2   (agg. 3-5)
     Botev Plovdiv v Etar Tarnovo   3-0 1-1   (agg. 4-1)

Final   **Levski Sofia** 2, Botev Plovdiv 1

TOP GOALSCORERS

21 Yordanov (L. Gorna Oriahovitsa)
18 Lechkov (Sliven)
    Mikhtarski (Levski Sofia)
17 Stoianov V. (Chernomorets B.)
15 Genchev B. (Etar Tarnovo)

EUROPEAN CUPS

Champions' Cup
CSKA SOFIA
1st round   KA (Iceland)
     A 0-1, H 3-0, (agg. 3-1)
2nd round   Bayern Munich
     (West Germany)
     A 0-4, H 0-3, (agg. 0-7)

Cup-winners' Cup
SLIVEN
1st round   Juventus (Italy)
     H 0-2, A 1-6, (agg. 1-8)

UEFA Cup
SLAVIA SOFIA
1st round   Omonia Nicosia
     (Cyprus)
     H 2-1, A 2-4, (agg. 4-5)

1991/92 Qualifiers
Champions' Cup   Etar Tarnovo
Cup-winners' Cup   Levski Sofia
UEFA Cup   CSKA Sofia
     Slavia Sofia

NATIONAL TEAM RESULTS 90-91

12/09/90	Switzerland (ECQ)	A	Geneva	0-2	
26/09/90	Sweden	A	Solna	0-2	
17/10/90	Romania (ECQ)	A	Bucharest	3-0	Sirakov, Todorov 2
14/11/90	Scotland (ECQ)	H	Sofia	1-1	Todorov
27/03/91	Scotland (ECQ)	A	Glasgow	1-1	Kostadinov
09/04/91	Denmark	A	Odense	1-1	Alexandrov
01/05/91	Switzerland (ECQ)	H	Sofia	2-3	Kostadinov, Sirakov
22/05/91	San Marino (ECQ)	A	Serravalle	3-0	Ivanov, Sirakov, Penev (pen)
29/05/91	Brazil	A	Uberaba	0-3	

CHAMPIONSHIP TABLE 90-91

		Pd	W	D	L	F	A	Pt	GD
1	APOLLON	26	19	6	1	60	20	44	+40
2	ANORTHOSIS	26	18	5	3	42	14	41	+28
3	APOEL	26	13	9	4	48	23	35	+25
4	OMONIA	26	12	7	7	41	22	31	+19
5	AEL	26	10	8	8	36	36	28	=
6	NEA SALAMIS	26	9	9	8	38	31	27	+7
7	PEZOPORIKOS	26	8	11	7	35	28	27	+7
8	ARIS	26	9	6	11	33	40	24	-7
9	ALKI	26	8	8	10	32	40	24	-8
10	EPA	26	7	10	9	29	37	24	-8
11	OLYMPIAKOS	26	7	9	10	36	37	23	-1
12	PARALIMNI	26	7	7	12	33	45	21	-12
14	APOP	26	1	4	21	20	63	6	-43
13	APEP	26	3	3	20	18	65	5	-47

N.B. APEP 4 points deducted

Relegated - APOP, APEP
Promoted - EVAGORAS, OMONIA ARADIPPOU

TOP GOALSCORERS

19	Xiourouppas	(Omonia)
	Besirevic	(Apollon)
17	Gogic	(Apoel)

EUROPEAN CUPS

Champions' Cup
APOEL
  1st round Bayern Munich
    (West Germany)
    H 2-3, A 0-4, (agg. 2-7)

Cup-winners' Cup
NEA SALAMIS
  1st round Aberdeen (Scotland)
    H 0-2, A 0-3, (agg. 0-5)

UEFA Cup
OMONIA
  1st round Slavia Sofia (Bulgaria)
    A 1-2, H 4-2, (agg. 5-4)
  2nd round Anderlecht (Belgium)
    H 1-1, A 0-3, (agg. 1-4)

1991/92 Qualifiers

Champions' Cup	Apollon
Cup-winners' Cup	Omonia
UEFA Cup	Anorthosis

DOMESTIC CUP 90-91

Quarters	Omonia v Akritas	2-0	3-0	(agg. 5-0)
	AEL v Apollon	0-0	2-1	(agg. 2-1)
	Ethnikos v Olympiakos	1-2	2-1	(agg. 3-3; 1-3 on pens)
	Pezoporikos v Aris	3-1	2-0	(agg. 5-1)
Semis	AEL v Olympiakos	0-0	1-2	(agg. 1-2)
	Pezoporikos v Omonia	1-0	0-1	(agg. 1-1; 2-4 on pens)
Final	Omonia 1, Olympiakos 0			

NATIONAL TEAM RESULTS 90-91

31/10/90	Hungary (ECQ)	A	Budapest	2-4	Xiourouppas, Tsolakis
14/11/90	Norway (ECQ)	H	Nicosia	0-3	
22/12/90	Italy (ECQ)	H	Limassol	0-4	
27/02/91	Greece	H	Limassol	1-1	Nicolaou
03/04/91	Hungary (ECQ)	H	Limassol	0-2	
01/05/91	Norway (ECQ)	A	Oslo	0-3	
29/05/91	USSR (ECQ)	A	Moscow	0-4	

CHAMPIONSHIP TABLE 90-91

		Pd	W	D	L	F	A	Pt	GD
1	SPARTA PRAGUE	30	15	9	6	58	28	39	+30
2	SLOVAN BRATIS'VA	30	16	6	8	47	27	38	+20
3	SIGMA OLOMOUC	30	16	5	9	52	34	37	+18
4	DUNAJSKA STREDA	30	12	11	7	39	36	35	+3
5	BANIK OSTRAVA	30	14	4	12	50	34	32	+16
6	UNION CHEB	30	13	6	11	44	36	32	+8
7	INTER BRATISLAVA	30	10	10	10	41	42	30	-1
8	DUKLA BANSKA B.	30	11	8	11	35	37	30	-2
9	SLAVIA PRAGUE	30	10	10	10	44	48	30	-4
10	TATRAN PRESOV	30	10	9	11	42	40	29	+2
11	DUKLA PRAGUE	30	12	5	13	38	52	29	-14
12	VITKOVICE	30	12	4	14	47	52	28	-5
13	BOHEMIANS PRAGUE	30	10	7	13	35	50	27	-15
14	HRADEC KRALOVE	30	10	7	13	33	52	27	-19
15	NITRA	30	9	7	14	30	35	25	-5
16	ZBROJOVKA BRNO	30	2	8	20	20	52	12	-32

Relegated - NITRA, ZBROJOVKA BRNO
Promoted - SPARTAK TRNAVA, DYNAMO CESKE BUDEJOVICE

DOMESTIC CUP 90-91

Semi-Finals	Sparta Prague	0	**Banik Ostrava**	1
(Czech)	**Dyn. C. Budejoice**	3	Dukla Prague	0
Semi-Finals	**FC Nitra**	3	Slovan Bratislava	1
(Slovak)	D. Banska Bystrica	1	**Spartak Trnava**	1
			(1-4 on pens.)	

Final (Czech)	**Banik Ostrava**	4	Dyn. C. Budejovice	2
Final (Slovak)	**Spartak Trnava**	1	FC Nitra	0

Final	**Banik Ostrava**	6	Spartak Trnava	1
(Czechoslovakian)				

TOP GOALSCORERS

17	Kukleta	(Sparta Prague)
15	Vytykac	(Tatran Presov)
14	Bartl	(Vitkovice)
13	Rusnak	(Dukla Banska Bystrica)
	Kuka	(Slavia Prague)

EUROPEAN CUPS

Champions' Cup
SPARTA PRAGUE
1st round   Spartak Moscow
             H 0-2, A 0-2, (agg. 0-4)
Cup-winners' Cup
DUKLA PRAGUE
1st round   Sliema Wanderers
             (Malta)
             A 2-1, H 2-0, (agg. 4-1)
2nd round   Dinamo Kiev (USSR)
             A 0-1, H 2-2, (agg. 2-3)

UEFA Cup
INTER BRATISLAVA
1st round   Avenir Beggen
             (Luxembourg)
             A 1-2, H 5-0, (agg. 6-2)
2nd round   Cologne (W. Germany)
             A 1-0, H 0-2, (agg. 1-2)
BANIK OSTRAVA
1st round   Aston Villa (England)
             A 1-3, H 1-2, (agg. 2-5)

1990/91 Qualifiers
Champions' Cup   Sparta Prague
Cup-winners' Cup Banik Ostrava
UEFA Cup   Slovan Bratislava
                  Sigma Olomouc

NATIONAL TEAM RESULTS 90-91

29/08/90	Finland	A	Kuusankoski	1-1	Kuka
26/09/90	Iceland (ECQ)	H	Kosice	1-0	Danek
13/10/90	France (ECQ)	A	Paris	1-2	Skuhravy
14/11/90	Spain (ECQ)	H	Prague	3-2	Danek 2, Moravcik
30/01/91	Australia	A	Melbourne	1-0	Kristofik
06/02/91	Australia	A	Sydney	2-0	Kula, Grussmann
27/03/91	Poland	H	Olomouc	4-0	Kuka, Moravcik, Pecko, Danek
01/05/91	Albania (ECQ)	A	Tirana	2-0	Kubik, Kuka
05/06/91	Iceland (ECQ)	A	Reykjavik	1-0	Hasek

DENMARK

CHAMPIONSHIP TABLE 90

		Pd	W	D	L	F	A	Pt	GD
1	BRONDBY	26	17	8	1	50	16	42	+34
2	B 1903	26	10	11	5	44	27	31	+17
3	IKAST	26	11	8	7	38	27	30	+11
4	SILKEBORG	26	11	8	7	35	26	30	+9
5	FREM	26	7	15	4	33	25	29	+8
6	LYNGBY	26	10	8	8	44	30	28	+14
7	AGF	26	9	10	7	31	25	28	+6
8	OB	26	9	9	8	32	28	27	+4
9	VEJLE	26	8	10	8	32	32	26	=
10	AAB	26	8	10	8	32	34	26	-2
11	NAESTVED	26	6	10	10	20	34	22	-14
12	HERFOLGE	26	4	9	13	21	47	17	-26
13	KB	26	4	6	16	24	52	14	-28
14	VIBORG	26	5	4	17	19	52	14	-33

Relegated - NAESTVED, HERFOLGE, KB, VIBORG
Promoted - none

CHAMPIONSHIP TABLE 91

		Pd	W	D	L	F	A	Pt	GD
1	BRONDBY	18	10	6	2	26	15	26	+11
2	LYNGBY	18	10	4	4	35	18	24	+17
3	AGF	18	6	8	4	29	26	20	+3
4	FREM	18	6	7	5	25	24	19	+1
5	OB	18	3	11	4	21	20	17	+1
6	AAB	18	6	5	7	29	33	17	-4
7	B 1903	18	6	4	8	19	18	16	+1
8	VEJLE	18	5	6	7	20	22	16	-2
9	SILKEBORG	18	4	7	7	23	33	15	-10
10	IKAST	18	3	4	11	9	27	10	-18

Relegated - IKAST   Promoted - NAESTVED

EUROPEAN CUPS

Champions' Cup
OB
| 1st round | Real Madrid (Spain) |
| | H 1-4, A 0-6, (agg. 1-10) |

Cup-winners' Cup
LYNGBY
| 1st round | Wrexham (Wales) |
| | A 0-0, H 0-1, (agg. 0-1) |

UEFA Cup
BRONDBY
1st round	Eintracht Frankfurt (West Germany)
	H 5-0, A 1-4, (agg. 6-4)
2nd round	Ferencvaros (Hungary)
	H 3-0, A 1-0, (agg. 4-0)
3rd round	Bayer Leverkusen (West Germany)
	H 3-0, A 0-0, (agg. 3-0)
Quarter	Torp. Moscow (USSR)
	H 1-0, A 0-1, (agg. 1-1; 4-2 on pens.)
Semi	Roma (Italy)
	H 0-0, A 1-2, (agg. 1-2)

VEJLE
| 1st round | Admira Wacker (Austria) |
| | H 0-1, A 0-3, (agg. 0-4) |

1991/92 Qualifiers
Champions' Cup   Brondby
Cup-winners' Cup OB
UEFA Cup   B 1903, Ikast

Domestic Cup Results and Top Scorers appear on page 12

NATIONAL TEAM RESULTS 90-91

05/09/90	Sweden	A	Vasteras	1-0	Christensen
11/09/90	Wales	H	Copenhagen	1-0	Laudrup B.
10/10/90	Faeroe Isles (ECQ)	H	Copenhagen	4-1	Laudrup M. 2, Elstrup, Povlsen
17/10/90	N. Ireland (ECQ)	A	Belfast	1-1	Bartram (pen)
14/11/90	Yugoslavia (ECQ)	H	Copenhagen	0-2	
09/04/91	Bulgaria	H	Odense	1-1	Hogh
01/05/91	Yugoslavia (ECQ)	A	Belgrade	2-1	Christensen 2
05/06/91	Austria (ECQ)	H	Odense	2-1	Christensen 2
12/06/91	Italy	N	Malmo	0-2	
15/06/91	Sweden	A	Norrkoping	0-4	

CHAMPIONSHIP TABLE 90-91

		Pd	W	D	L	F	A	Pt	GD
1	ARSENAL	38	24	13	1	74	18	83	+56
2	LIVERPOOL	38	23	7	8	77	40	76	+37
3	CRYSTAL PALACE	38	20	9	9	50	41	69	+9
4	LEEDS UNITED	38	19	7	12	65	47	64	+18
5	MANCHESTER CITY	38	17	11	10	64	53	62	+11
6	MANCHESTER UTD	38	16	12	10	58	45	59	+13
7	WIMBLEDON	38	14	14	10	53	46	56	+7
8	NOTT'M FOREST	38	14	12	12	65	50	54	+15
9	EVERTON	38	13	12	13	50	46	51	+4
10	TOTTENHAM	38	11	16	11	51	50	49	+1
11	CHELSEA	38	13	10	15	58	69	49	-11
12	QPR	38	12	10	16	44	53	46	-9
13	SHEFFIELD UNITED	38	13	7	18	36	55	46	-19
14	SOUTHAMPTON	38	12	9	17	58	69	45	-11
15	NORWICH CITY	38	13	6	19	41	64	45	-23
16	COVENTRY CITY	38	11	11	16	42	49	44	-7
17	ASTON VILLA	38	9	14	15	46	58	41	-12
18	LUTON TOWN	38	10	7	21	42	61	37	-19
19	SUNDERLAND	38	8	10	20	38	60	34	-22
20	DERBY COUNTY	38	5	9	24	37	75	24	-38

N.B. 3 pts for a win. ARSENAL 2 pts deducted; MANCHESTER UTD 1 pt deducted.

Relegated - SUNDERLAND, DERBY COUNTY

Promoted - OLDHAM ATHLETIC, WEST HAM UNITED,
SHEFFIELD WEDNESDAY, NOTTS COUNTY

TOP GOALSCORERS

22	Smith	(Arsenal)
21	Chapman	(Leeds United)
20	Quinn	(Manchester City)
	Fashanu	(Wimbledon)

EUROPEAN CUPS

Cup-winners' Cup
Manchester United

1st round	Pecs (Hungary)
	H 2-0, A 1-0, (agg. 3-0)
2nd round	Wrexham (Wales)
	H 3-0, A 2-0, (agg. 5-0)
Quarter	Montpellier (France)
	H 1-1, A 2-0, (agg. 3-1)
Semi	Legia Warsaw (Poland)
	A 3-1, H 1-1, (agg. 4-2)
Final	Barcelona (Spain), 2-1

UEFA Cup
Aston Villa

1st round	Banik Ostrava
	(Czechoslovakia)
	H 3-1, A 2-1, (agg. 5-2)
2nd round	Internazionale (Italy)
	H 2-0, A 0-3, (agg. 2-3)

1991/92 Qualifiers

Champions' Cup	Arsenal
Cup-winners' Cup	Manchester Utd
	Tottenham H.
UEFA Cup	Liverpool

Domestic Cup Results appear on page 12

NATIONAL TEAM RESULTS 90-91

12/09/90	Hungary	H	Wembley	1-0	Lineker
17/10/90	Poland (ECQ)	H	Wembley	2-0	Lineker (pen), Beardsley
14/11/90	Rep. Ireland (ECQ)	A	Dublin	1-1	Platt
06/02/91	Cameroon	H	Wembley	2-0	Lineker 2 (1 pen)
27/03/91	Rep. Ireland (ECQ)	H	Wembley	1-1	Staunton (og)
01/05/91	Turkey (ECQ)	A	Izmir	1-0	Wise
21/05/91	USSR	H	Wembley	3-1	Smith, Platt 2 (1 pen)
25/05/91	Argentina	H	Wembley	2-2	Lineker, Platt
01/06/91	Australia	A	Sydney	1-0	Gray (og)
03/06/91	New Zealand	A	Auckland	1-0	Lineker
09/06/91	New Zealand	A	Wellington	2-0	Pearce, Hirst
12/06/91	Malaysia	A	Kuala Lumpur	4-2	Lineker 4

FÆROE ISLES

CHAMPIONSHIP TABLE 90

		Pd	W	D	L	F	A	Pt	GD
1	HB	18	9	6	3	37	22	24	+15
2	B36	18	9	2	7	30	27	20	+3
3	MB	18	6	7	5	28	25	19	+3
4	GI	18	7	4	7	28	20	18	+8
5	VB	18	7	4	7	27	27	18	=
6	B68	18	6	6	6	19	20	18	-1
7	KI	18	6	5	7	30	36	17	-6
8	TB	18	7	2	9	21	26	16	-5
9	SIF	18	7	2	9	20	29	16	-9
10	B71	18	4	6	8	17	25	14	-8

Relegated – SIF, B71   Promoted – NSI, SUMBA

NATIONAL RESULTS 90-91

08/08/90	Iceland	H	Torshavn	2-3	Morkore K., Hansen O.
12/09/90	Austria (ECQ)	H	Landskrona	1-0	Nielsen
10/10/90	Denmark (ECQ)	A	Copenhagen	1-4	Morkore A.
01/05/91	N. Ireland (ECQ)	A	Belfast	1-1	Reynheim
16/05/91	Yugoslavia (ECQ)	A	Belgrade	0-7	
22/05/91	Austria (ECQ)	A	Salzburg	0-3	

TOP GOALSCORERS

10	Rasmussen	(MB)
	Mohr	(HB)
9	Nielsen	(SIF)
	Dalheim	(GI)

DOMESTIC CUP 90

Quarter-Finals

B71 v **MB**	2-3	
VB v **KI**	1-1	(5-6 on pens)
GI v LIF	6-1	
TB v B36	4-0	

Semi-Finals

TB v **GI**	3-1	1-4	(agg. 4-5)
MB v **KI**	0-3	3-2	(agg. 3-5)

Final

KI v GI	6-1

DENMARK

TOP SCORERS 90

17	Christensen B.	(Brondby)
16	Pedersen M.	(Ikast)
15	Frandsen	(B 1903)
14	Nielsen P.	(Lyngby)

TOP SCORERS 91

11	Christensen B.	(Brondby)
9	Pedersen P.	(Lyngby)
	Moller	(AaB)
8	Andersen S.	(AGF)
	Christensen F.	(Lyngby)

DOMESTIC CUP 90-91

Quarter-Finals	Brondby	1	Vejle	0	
	Olstykke	1	Ikast	1	(4-3 on pens.)
	Akademisk	2	**OB**	2	(2-5 on pens.)
	AaB	5	Herfolge	1	
Semi-Finals	**AaB** v Brondby	2-2	1-0		(agg. 3-2)
	OB v Olstykke	3-0	2-0		(agg. 5-0)
Final	AaB	0	OB	0	
(replay)	**OB**	0	AaB	0	
	(a.e.t. 4-3 on pens.)				

ENGLAND

DOMESTIC CUP 90/91

Quarter-Finals

Tottenham H	2	Notts County	1
Arsenal	2	Cambridge Utd	1
Norwich City	0	**Nottingham F.**	1
West Ham Utd	2	Everton	1

Semi-Finals

Tottenham H.	3	Arsenal	1
Nottingham F.	4	West Ham Utd	0

Final

Tottenham Hotspur 2
Nottingham Forest 1
(a.e.t.)

CHAMPIONSHIP TABLE 90

		Pd	W	D	L	F	A	Pt	GD
1	FC KUUSYSI	22	14	5	3	34	12	33	+22
2	ROPS	22	12	5	5	29	17	29	+12
3	HJK	22	11	6	5	40	29	28	+11
4	KUPS	22	8	8	6	24	22	24	+2
5	REIPAS	22	7	9	6	35	21	23	+14
6	TPS	22	7	9	6	27	20	23	+7
7	MP	22	6	11	5	20	22	23	-2
8	HAKA	22	8	6	8	27	34	22	-7
9	ILVES	22	6	8	8	37	33	20	+4
10	OTP	22	4	7	11	16	32	15	-16
11	KPV	22	6	3	13	15	32	15	-17
12	KUMU	22	1	7	14	13	43	9	-30

CHAMPIONSHIP PLAY-OFFS

Quarter-Finals	FC Kuusysi bt Haka	MP bt RoPS
	HJK bt TPS	Reipas bt KuPS
Semi-Finals	FC Kuusysi bt MP	HJK bt Reipas
Final	HJK bt FC Kuusysi	(HJK Champions)

Relegated	Promoted
KPV, KUMU	PPT, JARO

DOMESTIC CUP 90

Quarter-Finals	KuPS	4	KontU	0
	Ilves	1	RoPS	0
	Kumu	4	OTP	2
	Reipas	1	HJK	3
Semi-Finals	HJK	3	KuPS	1
	Kumu	1	Ilves	3
Final	Ilves	2	Haka	1

TOP GOALSCORERS

16	Czakon	(Ilves)
14	Litmanen	(Reipas)
13	Rajamaki	(TPS)
12	Tarkkio	(HJK)

EUROPEAN CUPS

Champions' Cup
FC KUUSYSI
1st round   FC Swarovski Tirol
(Austria)
A 0-5, H 1-2, (agg. 1-7)

Cup-winners' Cup
KUPS
1st round   Dinamo Kiev (USSR)
H 2-2, A 0-4, (agg. 2-6)

UEFA Cup
TPS
1st round   GKS Katowice (Poland)
A 0-3, H 0-1, (agg. 0-4)

RoPS
1st round   Magdeburg
(East Germany)
A 0-0, H 0-1, (agg. 0-1)

1991/92 Qualifiers

Champions' Cup	HJK
Cup-winners' Cup	Ilves
UEFA Cup	FC Kuusysi
	MP

NATIONAL TEAM RESULTS 90-91

29/08/90	Czechoslovakia	H	Kuusankoski	1-1	Jarvinen
12/09/90	Portugal (ECQ)	H	Helsinki	0-0	
11/11/90	Tunisia	A	Tunis	2-1	Paatelainen, Tegelberg
25/11/90	Malta (ECQ)	A	Ta' Qali	1-1	Holmgren
13/03/91	Poland	A	Warsaw	1-1	Paatelainen
17/04/91	Holland (ECQ)	A	Rotterdam	0-2	
16/05/91	Malta (ECQ)	H	Helsinki	2-0	Jarvinen, Litmanen
05/06/91	Holland (ECQ)	H	Helsinki	1-1	Holmgren

FRANCE

CHAMPIONSHIP TABLE 90-91

		Pd	W	D	L	F	A	Pt	GD
1	MARSEILLE	38	22	11	5	67	28	55	+39
2	MONACO	38	20	11	7	51	30	51	+21
3	AUXERRE	38	19	10	9	63	36	48	+27
4	CANNES	38	12	17	9	32	28	41	+4
5	LYON	38	15	11	12	39	44	41	-5
6	LILLE	38	11	17	10	39	37	39	+2
7	MONTPELLIER	38	12	14	12	44	35	38	+9
8	CAEN	38	13	12	13	38	36	38	+2
9	PARIS-ST-GERMAIN	38	13	12	13	40	42	38	-2
10	BORDEAUX	38	11	15	12	34	32	37	+2
11	BREST	38	11	15	12	45	46	37	-1
12	METZ	38	12	12	14	44	51	36	-7
13	SAINT-ETIENNE	38	13	9	16	40	46	35	-6
14	NICE	38	10	14	14	40	42	34	-2
15	NANTES	38	9	16	13	34	44	34	-10
16	TOULON	38	9	16	13	31	41	34	-10
17	NANCY	38	11	11	16	38	58	33	-20
18	SOCHAUX	38	8	16	14	24	33	32	-9
19	TOULOUSE	38	8	15	15	33	45	31	-12
20	RENNES	38	7	14	17	29	51	28	-22

Relegated - RENNES
BORDEAUX, BREST, NICE (Subject to appeal)
Promoted - LE HAVRE, NIMES

DOMESTIC CUP 90-91

Quarter-Finals	Nantes	1	**Marseille**	2
	Rodez	2	Sochaux	1
	Gueugnon	1	Niort	0
	Cannes	1	**Monaco**	2
Semi-Finals	**Monaco**	5	Gueugnon	0
	Marseille	4	Rodez	1
Final	**Monaco**	1	Marseille	0

NATIONAL TEAM 90-91

15/08/90	Poland	H	Paris	0-0	
05/09/90	Iceland (ECQ)	A	Rejkjavik	2-1	Papin, Cantona
13/10/90	C'slovakia (ECQ)	H	Paris	2-1	Papin 2
17/11/90	Albania (ECQ)	A	Tirana	1-0	Boli
20/02/91	Spain (ECQ)	H	Paris	3-1	Sauzee, Papin, Blanc
30/03/91	Albania (ECQ)	H	Paris	5-0	Sauzee 2, Papin 2 (1 pen), Lekbello (og)

TOP GOALSCORERS

23	Papin	(Marseille)
16	Kovacs	(Auxerre)

EUROPEAN CUPS

Champions' Cup
MARSEILLE

1st round	Dinamo Tirana (Albania) H 5-1, A 0-0, (agg. 5-1)
2nd round	Lech Poznan (Poland) A 2-3, H 6-1, (agg. 8-4)
Quarter	Milan (Italy) A 1-1, H 1-0 (later awarded 3-0), (agg. 4-1)
Semi	Spartak Moscow (USSR) A 3-1, H 2-1, (agg. 5-2)
Final	Red Star Belgrade (Yugoslavia) 0-0 (3-5 on pens.)

Cup-winners' Cup
MONTPELLIER

1st round	PSV (Holland) H 1-0, A 0-0, (agg. 1-0)
2nd round	Steaua Bucharest (Romania) H 5-0, A 3-0, (agg. 8-0)
Quarter	Manchester United (England) A 1-1, H 0-2, (agg. 1-3)

UEFA Cup
BORDEAUX

1st round	Glenavon (N. Ireland) A 0-0, H 2-0, (agg. 2-0)
2nd round	Magdeburg (East Germany) A 1-0, H 1-0, (agg. 2-0)
3rd round	Roma (Italy) A 0-5, H 0-2, (agg. 0-7)

MONACO

1st round	Roda JC (Holland) A 3-1, H 3-1, (agg. 6-2)
2nd round	Chernomorets Odessa (USSR) A 0-0, H 1-0, (agg. 1-0)
3rd round	Torpedo Moscow (USSR) A 1-2, H 1-0, (agg. 2-4)

1991/92 Qualifiers

Champions' Cup	Marseille
Cup-winners' Cup	Monaco
UEFA Cup	Auxerre, Cannes, Lyon

CHAMPIONSHIP TABLE 90-91

		Pd	W	D	L	F	A	Pt	GD
1	HANSA ROSTOCK	26	13	9	4	44	25	35	+19
2	DYNAMO DRESDEN	26	12	8	6	48	28	32	+20
3	ROT-WEISS ERFURT	26	11	9	6	30	26	31	+4
4	HFC CHEMIE	26	10	9	7	40	31	29	+9
5	CHEMNITZ	26	9	11	6	24	23	29	+1
6	CARL ZEISS JENA	26	12	4	10	41	36	28	+5
7	LOK. LEIPZIG	26	10	8	8	37	33	28	+4
8	BRANDENBURG	26	9	9	8	34	31	27	+3
9	EISENHUTTENSTADT	26	7	12	7	29	25	26	+4
10	MAGDEBURG	26	9	8	9	34	32	26	+2
11	FC BERLIN	26	7	8	11	25	39	22	-14
12	SACHSEN LEIPZIG	26	6	10	10	23	38	22	-15
13	ENERGIE COTTBUS	26	3	10	13	21	38	16	-17
14	VICT. FRANKFURT	26	4	5	17	29	54	13	-25

Promoted (to Bundesliga)
HANSA ROSTOCK, DYNAMO DRESDEN

Promoted (to 2nd Bundesliga)
ROT-WEISS ERFURT, HFC CHEMIE, CHEMNITZ, CARL ZEISS JENA, LOKOMOTIVE LEIPZIG, BRANDENBURG

DOMESTIC CUP 90-91

Quarters	Hansa Rostock	1	Rot-Weiss Erfurt	0
	Eisenhuttenstadt	1	Carl Zeiss Jena	0
	Lok. Leipzig	2	Stahl Brandenburg	0
	Union Berlin	1	Chemnitz	0
Semis	Eisenhuttenstadt	2	Union Berlin	0
	Lok. Leipzig	1	Hansa Rostock	1
	(1-3 on pens.)			
Final	Hansa Rostock	1	Eisenhuttenstadt	0

NATIONAL TEAM 90-91

12/09/90 Belgium A Brussels 2-0 Sammer 2

TOP GOALSCORERS

20	Gutschow	(Dynamo Dresden)
13	Schulbe	(HFC Chemie)
12	Fuchs	(Hansa Rostock)
10	Laessig	(Magdeburg)

EUROPEAN CUPS

Champions' Cup
DYNAMO DRESDEN

1st round	Union Luxembourg (Luxembourg) A 3-1, H 3-0, (agg. 6-1)
2nd round	Malmo (Sweden) H 1-1, A 1-1, (agg. 2-2; 5-4 on pens.)
Quarter	Red Star Belgrade (Yugoslavia) A 0-3, H 1-2 (later awarded 0-3), (agg. 0-6)

Cup-winners' Cup
PSV SCHWERIN

1st round	FK Austria (Austria) H 0-2, A 0-0, (agg. 0-2)

UEFA Cup
MAGDEBURG

1st round	RoPS (Finland) H 0-0, A 1-0, (agg. 1-0)
2nd round	Bordeaux (France) H 0-1, A 0-1, (agg. 0-2)

CHEMNITZ

1st round	Borussia Dortmund (West Germany) A 0-2, H 0-2, (agg. 0-4)

1991/92 Qualifiers

Champions' Cup	Hansa Rostock
Cup-winners' Cup	Eisenhuttenstadt
UEFA Cup	Rot-Weiss Erfurt
	HFC Chemie

CHAMPIONSHIP TABLE 90-91

		Pd	W	D	L	F	A	Pt	GD
1	KAISERSLAUTERN	34	19	10	5	72	45	48	+27
2	BAYERN MUNICH	34	18	9	7	74	41	45	+33
3	WERDER BREMEN	34	14	14	6	46	29	42	+17
4	EINTR. FRANKFURT	34	15	10	9	63	40	40	+23
5	HAMBURG	34	16	8	10	60	38	40	+22
6	VFB STUTTGART	34	14	10	10	57	44	38	+13
7	COLOGNE	34	13	11	10	50	43	37	+7
8	BAYER LEVERKUSEN	34	11	13	10	47	46	35	+1
9	BOR. M'GLADBACH	34	9	17	8	49	54	35	-5
10	BOR. DORTMUND	34	10	14	10	46	57	34	-11
11	WATTENSCHEID	34	9	15	10	42	51	33	-9
12	FORT. DUSSELDORF	34	11	10	13	40	49	32	-9
13	KARLSRUHE	34	8	15	11	46	52	31	-6
14	VFL BOCHUM	34	9	11	14	50	52	29	-2
15	NUREMBERG	34	10	9	15	40	54	29	-14
16	ST. PAULI	34	6	15	13	33	53	27	-20
17	BAYER UERDINGEN	34	5	13	16	34	54	23	-20
18	HERTHA BERLIN	34	3	8	23	37	84	14	-47

Relegated - ST. PAULI, BAYER UERDINGEN, HERTHA BERLIN
Promoted - SCHALKE 04, MSV DUISBURG, STUTTGARTER K.

DOMESTIC CUP 90-91

Quarters	Eintracht Frankfurt	3	Wattenscheid	1
	Hessen Kassel	0	**Werder Bremen**	2
	Cologne	1	VfB Stuttgart	0
	Bayer Uerdingen	1	**MSV Duisburg**	4

Semis	MSV Duisburg	0	Cologne	0
(replay)	**Cologne**	3	MSV Duisburg	0
	Eintracht Frankfurt	2	Werder Bremen	2
(replay)	**Werder Bremen**	6	Eintracht Frankfurt	3

Final	**Werder Bremen**	1	Cologne	1
	(a.e.t. 4-3 on pens.)			

TOP GOALSCORERS

21	Wohlfarth	(Bayern Munich)
20	Furtok	(Hamburg)
16	Moller	(Eintracht Frankfurt)
15	Rufer	(Werder Bremen)
	Allofs	(Fortuna Dusseldorf)

National Team Results appear on page 28

EUROPEAN CUPS

Champions' Cup
BAYERN MUNICH

1st round	Apoel (Cyprus)
	A 3-2, H 4-0, (agg. 7-2)
2nd round	CSKA Sofia (Bulgaria)
	H 4-0, A 3-0, (agg. 7-0)
Quarter	FC Porto (Portugal)
	H 1-1, A 2-0, (agg. 3-1)
Semi	Red Star Belgrade (Yugoslavia)
	H 1-2, A 2-2, (agg. 3-4)

Cup-winners' Cup
KAISERSLAUTERN

1st round	Sampdoria (Italy)
	H 1-0, A 0-2, (agg. 1-2)

UEFA Cup
EINTRACHT FRANKFURT

1st round	Brondby (Denmark)
	A 0-5, H 4-1, (agg. 4-6)

COLOGNE

1st round	IFK Norrkoping (Sweden)
	A 0-0, H 3-1, (agg. 3-1)
2nd round	Inter Bratislava (Czechoslovakia)
	H 0-1, A 2-0, (agg. 2-1)
3rd round	Atalanta (Italy)
	H 1-1, A 0-1, (agg. 1-2)

BORUSSIA DORTMUND

1st round	Chemnitz (East Germany)
	H 2-0, A 2-0, (agg. 4-0)
2nd round	Universitatea Craiova (Romania)
	A 3-0, H 1-0, (agg. 4-0)
3rd round	Anderlecht (Belgium)
	A 0-1, H 2-1, (agg. 2-2; lost on away goals)

BAYER LEVERKUSEN

1st round	FC Twente (Holland)
	H 1-0, A 1-1, (agg. 2-1)
2nd round	GKS Katowice (Poland)
	A 2-1, H 4-0, (agg. 6-1)
3rd round	Brondby (Denmark)
	A 0-3, H 0-0, (agg. 0-3)

1991/92 Qualifiers

Champions' Cup	Kaiserslautern
Cup-winners' Cup	Werder Bremen
UEFA Cup	Bayern Munich
	Ein. Frankfurt
	Hamburg
	VfB Stuttgart

CHAMPIONSHIP TABLE 90-91

		Pd	W	D	L	F	A	Pt	GD
1	PANATHINAIKOS	34	23	8	3	77	22	54	+55
2	OLYMPIAKOS	34	19	10	5	77	28	46	+49
3	AEK	34	18	6	10	59	33	42	+26
4	PAOK	34	16	9	9	56	39	38	+17
5	IRAKLIS	34	14	9	11	40	36	37	+4
6	ATHINAIKOS	34	16	5	13	40	33	37	+7
7	DOXA	34	14	6	14	42	45	34	-3
8	OFI	34	11	12	11	37	38	34	-1
9	ARIS	34	11	11	12	34	38	33	-4
10	PANIONIOS	34	9	12	13	38	54	30	-16
11	APOLLON	34	10	10	14	41	62	30	-21
12	LARISSA	34	10	9	15	38	46	29	-8
13	PANAHAIKI	34	9	10	15	36	48	28	-12
14	PANSERRAIKOS	34	9	10	15	30	42	28	-12
15	XANTHI	34	9	10	15	35	53	28	-18
16	IONIKOS	34	9	9	16	37	50	27	-13
17	LEVADIAKOS	34	10	7	17	35	51	27	-16
18	YANNINA	34	8	9	17	20	54	25	-34

N.B. PAOK 3 pts deducted; OLYMPIAKOS 2 pts deducted.

Relegated - IONIKOS, LEVADIAKOS, YANNINA
Promoted - ETHNIKOS, KORINTHOS, PIERIKOS

DOMESTIC CUP 90-91

Quarters	PAOK v Larissa	3-0 0-2 (agg. 3-2)
	Athinaikos v Doxa	2-0 1-0 (agg. 3-0)
	Ionikos v Panathinaikos	0-3 1-3 (agg. 1-6)
	Panionios v OFI	2-0 0-2 (agg. 2-2; 3-2 on pens.)
Semis	Panathinaikos v PAOK	2-0 0-1 (agg. 2-1)
	Athinaikos v Panionios	3-0 1-3 (agg. 4-3)
Final	Athinaikos v Panathinaikos	0-3 1-2 (agg. 1-5)

TOP GOALSCORERS

23 Saravakos (Panathinaikos)
18 Warzycha (Panathinaikos)
16 Anastopoulos (Olympiakos)
15 Vaitsis (Panahaiki)

EUROPEAN CUPS

Champions' Cup
PANATHINAIKOS
1st round Lech Poznan (Poland) A 0-3, H 1-2, (agg. 1-5)

Cup-winners' Cup
OLYMPIAKOS
1st round Flamurtari Vlora (Albania) H 3-1, A 2-0, (agg. 5-1)
2nd round Sampdoria (Italy) H 0-1, A 1-3, (agg. 1-4)

UEFA Cup
PAOK
1st round Sevilla (Spain) A 0-0, H 0-0, (agg. 0-0; 3-4 on pens)
IRAKLIS
1st round Valencia (Spain) H 0-0, A 0-2, (agg. 0-2)

1991/92 Qualifiers
Champions' Cup Panathinaikos
Cup-winners' Cup Athinaikos
UEFA Cup AEK, PAOK

NATIONAL TEAM RESULTS 90-91

05/09/90	Albania	H	Patras	1-0	Dimitriadis
10/10/90	Egypt	H	Athens	6-1	Tsalouhidis, Saravakos 5 (3pens)
31/10/90	Malta (ECQ)	H	Athens	4-0	Tsiantakis, Karapialis, Saravakos, Borbokis
21/11/90	Holland (ECQ)	A	Rotterdam	0-2	
18/12/90	Poland	H	Volos	1-2	Tsalouhidis
23/01/91	Portugal (ECQ)	H	Athens	3-2	Borbokis, Manolas, Tsalouhidis
27/02/91	Cyprus	A	Limassol	1-1	Saravakos
27/03/91	Morocco	A	Rabat	0-0	
17/04/91	Sweden	H	Athens	2-2	Vonderburg (og), Borbokis

CHAMPIONSHIP TABLE 90-91

		Pd	W	D	L	F	A	Pt	GD
1	PSV	34	23	7	4	84	28	53	+56
2	AJAX	34	22	9	3	75	21	53	+54
3	FC GRONINGEN	34	18	10	6	62	38	46	+24
4	FC UTRECHT	34	16	10	8	42	29	42	+13
5	VITESSE	34	11	15	8	39	32	37	+7
6	FC TWENTE	34	13	10	11	58	48	36	+10
7	RKC	34	11	13	10	51	49	35	+2
8	FEYENOORD	34	8	16	10	39	40	32	-1
9	FC VOLENDAM	34	10	12	12	37	45	32	-8
10	RODA JC	34	12	7	15	40	53	31	-13
11	WILLEM II	34	13	4	17	53	50	30	+3
12	FORTUNA SITTARD	34	9	12	13	33	47	30	-14
13	SPARTA	34	7	15	12	40	57	29	-17
14	FC DEN HAAG	34	10	8	16	40	60	28	-20
15	MVV	34	9	9	16	38	56	27	-18
16	SVV	34	8	8	18	31	52	24	-21
17	SC HEERENVEEN	34	9	6	19	41	63	24	-22
18	NEC	34	6	11	17	27	62	23	-35

Relegated - SC HEERENVEEN, NEC
Promoted - DE GRAAFSCHAP, VVV

DOMESTIC CUP 90-91

Quarters	Roda JC	1	Ajax	0	
	Willem II	2	**PSV**	3	
	BVV Den Bosch	0	Vitesse	0	(4-3 on pens.)
	Dordrecht 90	1	**Feyenoord**	3	
Semis	BVV Den Bosch	2	Roda JC	2	(4-1 on pens.)
	PSV	0	**Feyenoord**	1	
Final	**Feyenoord**	1	BVV Den Bosch	0	

(second half to be replayed, by Civil Court order)

TOP GOALSCORERS

25	Romario	(PSV)
	Bergkamp	(Ajax)
17	Stewart	(Willem II)

EUROPEAN CUPS

Cup-winners' Cup
PSV
1st round Montpellier (France)
A 0-1, H 0-0, (agg. 0-1)

UEFA Cup
RODA JC
1st round Monaco (France)
H 1-3, A 1-3, (agg. 2-6)

FC TWENTE
1st round Bayer Leverkusen
(West Germany)
A 0-1, H 1-1, (agg. 1-2)

VITESSE
1st round Derry City
(Republic of Ireland)
A 1-0, H 0-0, (agg. 1-0)
2nd round Dundee United
(Scotland)
H 1-0, A 4-0, (agg. 5-0)
3rd round Sporting (Portugal)
H 0-2, A 1-2, (agg. 1-4)

1991/92 Qualifiers
Champions' Cup   PSV
Cup-winners' Cup Feyenoord
UEFA Cup   Ajax
                 FC Groningen
                 FC Utrecht

NATIONAL TEAM RESULTS 90-91

26/09/90	Italy	A	Palermo	0-1	
17/10/90	Portugal (ECQ)	A	Oporto	0-1	
21/11/90	Greece (ECQ)	H	Rotterdam	2-0	Bergkamp, Van Basten
19/12/90	Malta (ECQ)	A	Ta' Qali	8-0	Van Basten 5 (1 pen), Winter, Bergkamp 2
13/03/91	Malta (ECQ)	H	Rotterdam	1-0	Van Basten (pen)
17/04/91	Finland (ECQ)	H	Rotterdam	2-0	Van Basten, Gullit
05/06/91	Finland (ECQ)	A	Helsinki	1-1	De Boer

CHAMPIONSHIP TABLE 90-91

		Pd	W	D	L	F	A	Pt	GD
1	HONVED	30	19	7	4	50	20	45	+30
2	FERENCVAROS	30	15	10	5	47	22	40	+25
3	PECS	30	15	7	8	32	20	37	+12
4	VACI IZZO	30	14	8	8	35	29	36	+6
5	VESZPREM	30	11	12	7	34	25	34	+9
6	TATABANYA	30	12	9	9	37	32	33	+5
7	SIOFOK	30	10	11	9	25	28	31	-3
8	VIDEOTON	30	11	8	11	39	41	30	-2
9	UJPESTI TE	30	13	4	13	36	39	30	-3
10	MTK-VM	30	10	6	14	38	39	26	-1
11	RABA ETO	30	8	10	12	35	41	26	-6
12	VASAS	30	8	8	14	32	43	24	-11
13	SZEGED	30	9	6	15	26	37	24	-11
14	DEBRECEN	30	7	8	15	27	40	22	-13
15	BEKESCSABA	30	7	7	16	24	39	21	-15
16	VOLAN	30	8	5	17	28	50	21	-22

Relegated - SZEGED, DEBRECEN, BEKESCSABA, VOLAN
Promoted - BVSC, HALADAS, DIOSGYOR, ZALAEGERSZEG

DOMESTIC CUP 90-91

Quarters	Tatabanya v **Kazincbarcika**	0-0	1-2	(agg. 1-2)
	Vaci Izzo v Dorog	1-1	2-2	(agg. 3-3; Vaci Izzo on away goals)
	Volan v **Ferencvaros**	0-3	2-1	(agg. 2-4)
	Paksi Atom v **Diosgyor**	0-0	1-0	(agg. 1-0)
Semis	**Ferencvaros** v Paksi Atom	4-0	1-2	(agg. 5-2)
	Kazincbarcika v **Vaci Izzo**	0-1	0-0	(agg. 0-1)
Final	**Ferencvaros** 1	Vaci Izzo 0		

TOP GOALSCORERS

15	Gregor	(Honved)
12	Fischer	(Ferencvaros)
11	Vaczi	(Tatabanya)
10	Belansky	(Pecs)

EUROPEAN CUPS

Champions' Cup
UJPESTI DOZSA
| 1st round | Napoli (Italy) |
| | A 0-3, H 0-2, (agg. 0-5) |

Cup-winners' Cup
PECS
| 1st round | Manchester United (England) |
| | A 0-2, H 0-1, (agg. 0-3) |

UEFA Cup
MTK-VM
| 1st round | Luzern (Switzerland) |
| | H 1-1, A 1-2, (agg. 2-3) |

FERENCVAROS
1st round	Antwerp (Belgium)
	A 0-0, H 3-1, (agg. 3-1)
2nd round	Brondby (Denmark)
	A 0-3, H 0-1, (agg. 0-4)

1991/92 Qualifiers
Champions' Cup	Honved
Cup-winners' Cup	Ferencvaros
UEFA Cup	Pecs
	Vaci Izzo

NATIONAL TEAM RESULTS 90-91

05/09/90	Turkey	H	Budapest	4-1	Kovacs, Kozma, Kiprich 2 (1pen)
12/09/90	England	A	Wembley	0-1	
10/10/90	Norway (ECQ)	A	Bergen	0-0	
17/10/90	Italy (ECQ)	H	Budapest	1-1	Disztl
31/10/90	Cyprus (ECQ)	H	Budapest	4-2	Lorincz, Christodoulou (og), Kiprich 2 (2 pens)
19/02/91	Argentina	A	Rosario	0-2	
27/03/91	Spain	A	Santander	4-2	Kiprich 2, Lorincz 2
03/04/91	Cyprus (ECQ)	A	Limassol	2-0	Szalma, Kiprich
17/04/91	USSR (ECQ)	H	Budapest	0-1	
01/05/91	Italy (ECQ)	A	Salerno	1-3	Bognar (pen)

CHAMPIONSHIP TABLE 90

		Pd	W	D	L	F	A	Pt	GD
1	FRAM	18	12	2	4	39	16	38	+23
2	KR	18	12	2	4	31	17	38	+14
3	IBV	18	11	4	3	39	32	37	+7
4	VALUR	18	10	3	5	29	21	33	+8
5	STJARNAN	18	8	2	8	25	27	26	-2
6	FH	18	7	2	9	24	29	23	-5
7	VIKINGUR	18	4	7	7	17	24	19	-7
8	KA	18	5	1	12	18	28	16	-10
9	THOR	18	4	3	11	13	24	15	-11
10	IA	18	3	2	13	19	36	11	-17

N.B. 3 points for a win

Relegated - THOR, IA   Promoted - VIDIR, UBK

DOMESTIC CUP 90

Quarter-Finals	Vikingur	2	Stjarnan	1
	Valur	2	UBK	0
	KR	3	IA	0
	IBK	3	Selfoss	2
Semi-Finals	IBK	2	KR	4
	Valur	2	Vikingur	0
Final	Valur	1	KR	1
(replay)	Valur	0	KR	0 (5-4 on pens)

NATIONAL TEAM 90-91

08/08/90	Faeroe Isles	A	Torshavn	3-2	Gregory 2, Gudjohnsen (pen)
05/09/90	France (ECQ)	H	Reykjavik	1-2	Edvaldsson
26/09/90	C'slovakia (ECQ)	A	Kosice	0-1	
10/10/90	Spain (ECQ)	A	Seville	1-2	Jonsson Si.
27/04/91	England B	A	Watford	0-1	
01/05/91	Wales	A	Cardiff	0-1	
26/05/91	Albania (ECQ)	A	Tirana	0-1	
05/06/91	C'slovakia (ECQ)	H	Reykjavik	0-1	

TOP GOALSCORERS

13	Magnusson	(FH)
10	Margeirsson	(KR)
	Steinsson	(Fram)
9	Stefansson	(IBV)

EUROPEAN CUPS

Champions' Cup
KA
1st round	CSKA Sofia (Bulgaria)
	H 1-0, A 0-3, (agg. 1-3)

Cup-winners' Cup
Fram
1st round	Djurgarden (Sweden)
	H 3-0, A 1-1, (agg. 4-1)
2nd round	Barcelona (Spain)
	H 1-2, A 0-3, (agg. 1-5)

UEFA Cup
FH
1st round	Dundee United (Scotland)
	H 1-3, A 2-2, (agg. 3-5)

1990/91 Qualifiers
Champions' Cup	Fram
Cup-winners' Cup	Valur
UEFA Cup	KR

CHAMPIONSHIP TABLE 90-91

		Pd	W	D	L	F	A	Pt	GD
1	SAMPDORIA	34	20	11	3	57	24	51	+33
2	MILAN	34	18	10	6	46	19	46	+27
3	INTERNAZIONALE	34	18	10	6	56	31	46	+25
4	GENOA	34	14	12	8	51	36	40	+15
5	TORINO	34	12	14	8	40	29	38	+11
6	PARMA	34	13	12	9	35	31	38	+4
7	JUVENTUS	34	13	11	10	45	32	37	+13
8	NAPOLI	34	11	15	8	37	37	37	=
9	ROMA	34	11	14	9	43	37	36	+6
10	ATALANTA	34	11	13	10	38	37	35	+1
11	LAZIO	34	8	19	7	33	36	35	-3
12	FIORENTINA	34	8	15	11	40	34	31	+6
13	BARI	34	9	11	14	41	47	29	-6
14	CAGLIARI	34	6	17	11	29	44	29	-15
15	LECCE	34	6	13	15	20	47	25	-27
16	PISA	34	8	6	20	34	60	22	-26
17	CESENA	34	5	9	20	28	58	19	-30
18	BOLOGNA	34	4	10	20	29	63	18	-34

Relegated - LECCE, PISA, CESENA, BOLOGNA
Promoted - FOGGIA, VERONA, CREMONESE, ASCOLI

DOMESTIC CUP 90-91

Quarter-Finals	**Napoli** v Bologna	0-1	3-1	(agg. 3-2)
	Torino v **Sampdoria**	1-0	0-1	(agg. 1-1; 2-3 on pens.)
	Roma v Juventus	1-1	2-0	(agg. 3-1)
	Bari v **Milan**	0-1	0-0	(agg. 0-1)
Semi-Finals	Napoli v **Sampdoria**	1-0	0-2	(agg. 1-2)
	Milan v **Roma**	0-0	0-1	(agg. 0-1)
Final	**Roma** v Sampdoria	3-1	1-1	(agg. 4-2)

TOP GOALSCORERS

19	Vialli	(Sampdoria)
16	Matthaus	(Internazionale)
15	Aguilera	(Genoa)
	Skuhravy	(Genoa)
14	Ciocci	(Cesena)
	Klinsmann	(Internazionale)
	Baggio	(Juventus)

SAN MARINO

NATIONAL TEAM RESULTS 90-91

14/11/90   H   Serravalle
Switzerland (ECQ) 0-4

05/12/90   A   Bucharest
Romania (ECQ)   0-6

27/03/91   H   Serravalle
Romania (ECQ)   1-3
                Pasolini (pen)

01/05/91   H   Serravalle
Scotland (ECQ)   0-2

22/05/91   H   Serravalle
Bulgaria (ECQ)   0-3

05/06/91   A   St. Gallen
Switzerland (ECQ) 0-7

NATIONAL TEAM RESULTS 90-91

Date	Opponent		Venue	Score	Scorers
26/09/90	Holland	H	Palermo	1-0	Baggio
17/10/90	Hungary (ECQ)	A	Budapest	1-1	Baggio (pen)
03/11/90	USSR (ECQ)	H	Rome	0-0	
22/12/90	Cyprus (ECQ)	A	Limassol	4-0	Vierchowod, Serena 2, Lombardo
13/02/91	Belgium	H	Terni	0-0	
01/05/91	Hungary (ECQ)	H	Salerno	3-1	Donadoni 2, Vialli
05/06/91	Norway (ECQ)	A	Oslo	1-2	Schillaci
12/06/91	Denmark	N	Malmo	2-0	Rizzitelli, Vialli
16/06/91	USSR	N	Solna	1-1	Giannini

EUROPEAN CUPS

Champions' Cup
MILAN

1st round	bye
2nd round	Club Bruges (Belgium)
	H 0-0, A 1-0, (agg. 1-0)
Quarter	Marseille (France)
	H 1-1, A 0-1 (later awarded 0-3),
	(agg. 1-4)

NAPOLI

1st round	Ujpesti Dozsa (Hungary)
	H 3-0, A 2-0, (agg. 5-0)
2nd round	Spartak Moscow (USSR)
	H 0-0, A 0-0, (agg. 0-0; 3-5 on pens)

Cup-winners' Cup
SAMPDORIA

1st round	Kaiserslautern (West Germany)
	A 0-1, H 2-0, (agg. 2-1)
2nd round	Olympiakos (Greece)
	A 1-0, H 3-1, (agg. 4-1)
Quarter	Legia Warsaw (Poland)
	A 0-1, H 2-2, (agg. 2-3)

JUVENTUS

1st round	Sliven (Bulgaria)
	A 2-0, H 6-1, (agg. 8-1)
2nd round	FK Austria (Austria)
	A 4-0, H 4-0, (agg. 8-0)
Quarter	FC Liege (Belgium)
	A 3-1, H 3-0, (agg. 6-1)
Semi	Barcelona (Spain)
	A 1-3, H 1-0, (agg. 2-3)

UEFA Cup
INTERNAZIONALE

1st round	Rapid Vienna (Austria)
	A 1-2, H 3-1, (agg. 4-3)
2nd round	Aston Villa (England)
	A 0-2, H 3-0, (agg. 3-2)
3rd round	Partizan Belgrade (Yugoslavia)
	H 3-0, A 1-1, (agg. 4-1)
Quarter	Atalanta (Italy)
	A 0-0, H 2-0, (agg. 2-0)
Semi	Sporting (Portugal)
	A 0-0, H 2-0, (agg. 2-0)
Final	Roma (Italy)
	H 2-0, A 0-1, (agg. 2-1)

ROMA

1st round	Benfica (Portugal)
	H 1-0, A 1-0, (agg. 2-0)
2nd round	Valencia (Spain)
	A 1-1, H 2-1, (agg. 3-2)
3rd round	Bordeaux (France)
	H 5-0, A 2-0, (agg. 7-0)
Quarter	Anderlecht (Belgium)
	H 3-0, A 3-2, (agg. 6-2)
Semi	Brondby (Denmark)
	A 0-0, H 2-1, (agg. 2-1)
Final	Internazionale (Italy)
	A 0-2, H 1-0, (agg. 1-2)

ATALANTA

1st round	Dinamo Zagreb (Yugoslavia)
	H 0-0, A 1-1, (agg. 1-1;
	won on away goals)
2nd round	Fenerbahce (Turkey)
	A 1-0, H 4-1, (agg. 5-1)
3rd round	Cologne (West Germany)
	A 1-1, H 1-0, (agg. 2-1)
Quarter	Internazionale (Italy)
	H 0-0, A 0-2, (agg. 0-2)

BOLOGNA

1st round	Zaglebie Lubin (Poland)
	A 1-0, H 1-0, (agg. 2-0)
2nd round	Hearts (Scotland)
	A 1-3, H 3-0, (agg. 4-3)
3rd round	Admira Wacker (Austria)
	A 0-3, H 3-0, (agg. 3-3; 6-5 on pens.)
Quarter	Sporting (Portugal)
	H 1-1, A 0-2, (agg. 1-3)

1991/92 Qualifiers

Champions' Cup	Sampdoria
Cup-winners' Cup	Roma
UEFA Cup	Internazionale
	Genoa
	Torino
	Parma

CHAMPIONSHIP TABLE 90-91

		Pd	W	D	L	F	A	Pt	GD
1	UNION	28	19	5	4	61	22	28	+39
2	JEUNESSE ESCH	28	14	9	5	48	31	25	+17
3	SPORA	28	15	4	9	51	41	22.5	+10
4	AVENIR BEGGEN	28	14	4	10	56	38	22	+18
5	GREVENMACHER	28	12	2	14	42	49	16	-7
6	HESPERANGE	28	9	6	13	48	52	14.5	-4
7	RED BOYS	18	9	0	9	28	30	18	-2
8	NIEDERCORN	18	6	3	9	23	33	15	-10
9	FOLA ESCH	18	4	1	13	10	40	9	-30
10	ARIS BONNEVOIE	18	0	2	16	7	38	2	-31

N.B. After 18 matches the top eight play off for the title, taking half their points total. The bottom four enter two promotion/relegation play-off groups with the top eight Second Division teams.

Relegated - NIEDERCORN, FOLA ESCH
Promoted - FC WILTZ, WORMELDANGE

TOP GOALSCORERS

23	Morocutti	(Union)
19	Thome	(Jeunesse Esch)
15	Reiter	(Spora)
14	Wagner	(Grevenmacher)
13	Horn	(Grevenmacher)

EUROPEAN CUPS

Champions' Cup
UNION LUXEMBOURG
1st round   Dynamo Dresden
(East Germany)
H 1-3, A 0-3, (agg. 1-6)

Cup-winners' Cup
SWIFT HESPERANGE
1st round   Legia Warsaw (Poland)
A 0-3, H 0-3, (agg. 0-6)

UEFA Cup
AVENIR BEGGEN
1st round   Inter Bratislava
(Czechoslovakia)
H 2-1, A 0-5, (agg. 2-6)

1991/92 Qualifiers
Champions' Cup   Union Luxembourg
Cup-winners' Cup Jeunesse Esch
UEFA Cup   Spora Luxembourg

DOMESTIC CUP 90-91

Quarters	Tricolore Gasperich	0	**Avenir Beggen**	3
	Swift Hesperange	2	CS Grevenmacher	0
	Union Luxembourg	2	Spora Luxembourg	0
	Jeunesse Esch	3	Red Boys Differdange	1
Semis	Avenir Beggen	0	**Union Luxembourg**	4
	Swift Hesperange	1	**Jeunesse Esch**	2
Final	**Union Luxembourg**	3	Jeunesse Esch	0

NATIONAL TEAM RESULTS 90-91

31/10/90	Germany (ECQ)	H	Luxembourg	2-3	Girres, Langers
14/11/90	Wales (ECQ)	H	Luxembourg	0-1	
27/02/91	Belgium (ECQ)	A	Brussels	0-3	

CHAMPIONSHIP TABLE 90-91

		Pd	W	D	L	F	A	Pt	GD
1	HAMRUN SPARTANS	16	10	4	2	31	18	24	+13
2	VALLETTA	16	8	3	5	28	17	19	+11
3	FLORIANA	16	6	6	4	15	11	18	+4
4	HIBERNIANS	16	5	7	4	18	15	17	+3
5	SLIEMA WANDERERS	16	4	7	5	24	20	15	+4
6	RABAT AJAX	16	4	6	6	18	19	14	-1
7	ZURRIEQ	16	4	6	6	12	19	14	-7
8	BIRKIRKARA	16	3	7	6	13	22	13	-9
9	NAXXAR LIONS	16	3	4	9	11	29	10	-18

Relegated - NAXXAR LIONS
Promoted - MQABBA HAJDUKS, ST. ANDREW'S

DOMESTIC CUP 90-91

Quarter-Finals	Sliema Wanderers	3	Hibernians	1
	Hamrun Spartans	2	Zurrieq	1
	Floriana	2	Rabat Ajax	0
	Valletta	4	St. George's	0
Semi-Finals	Valletta	2	Hamrun Spartans	1
	Sliema Wanderers	4	Floriana	1
Final	Valletta	2	Sliema Wanderers	1

NATIONAL TEAM 90-91

31/10/90	Greece (ECQ)	A	Athens	0-4	
25/11/90	Finland (ECQ)	H	Ta' Qali	1-1	Suda
19/12/90	Holland (ECQ)	H	Ta' Qali	0-8	
09/02/91	Portugal (ECQ)	H	Ta' Qali	0-1	
20/02/91	Portugal (ECQ)	A	Oporto	0-5	
13/03/91	Holland (ECQ)	A	Rotterdam	0-1	
16/05/91	Finland (ECQ)	A	Helsinki	0-2	

TOP GOALSCORERS

12	Zarb	(Valletta)
7	Scott	(Hibernians)
	Zerafa	(Valletta)
6	Brincat E.	(Hamrun Spartans)
	Gregory	(Sliema Wanderers)
	Suda	(Sliema Wanderers)

EUROPEAN CUPS

Champions' Cup
VALLETTA
1st round   Rangers (Scotland)
H 0-4, A 0-6, (agg. 0-10)

Cup-winners' Cup
SLIEMA WANDERERS
1st round   Dukla Prague
(Czechoslovakia)
H 1-2, A 0-2, (agg. 1-4)

UEFA Cup
HIBERNIANS
1st round   Partizan Belgrade
(Yugoslavia)
H 0-3, A 0-2, (agg. 0-5)

1991/92 Qualifiers
Champions' Cup   Hamrun Spartans
Cup-winners' Cup Valletta
UEFA Cup   Floriana

CHAMPIONSHIP TABLE 90-91

		Pd	W	D	L	F	A	Pt	GD
1	PORTADOWN	30	22	5	3	61	22	71	+39
2	BANGOR	30	19	4	7	51	29	61	+22
3	GLENTORAN	30	18	6	6	50	31	60	+19
4	GLENAVON	30	17	6	7	63	38	57	+25
5	NEWRY TOWN	30	15	5	10	50	42	50	+8
6	CLIFTONVILLE	30	14	7	9	59	41	49	+18
7	LINFIELD	30	12	10	8	40	34	46	+6
8	BALLYMENA UNITED	30	12	8	10	49	46	44	+3
9	ARDS	30	12	7	11	47	40	43	+7
10	CRUSADERS	30	11	9	10	53	46	42	+7
11	DISTILLERY	30	10	5	15	46	57	35	-11
12	OMAGH TOWN	30	10	4	16	47	65	34	-18
13	LARNE	30	8	6	16	41	59	30	-18
14	BALLYCLARE C'DES	30	5	6	19	33	67	21	-34
15	CARRICK RANGERS	30	4	5	21	30	58	17	-28
16	COLERAINE	30	2	5	23	25	70	11	-45

N.B. 3 points for a win

Relegated - none   Promoted - none

DOMESTIC CUP 90-91

Quarter-Finals	Ards	3	Linfield	2
	Crusaders	2	**Portadown**	4
	Glenavon	4	Ballyclare Comrades	0
	Larne	1	Glentoran	1
(replay)	**Glentoran**	4	Larne	1
Semi-Finals	**Portadown**	2	Ards	0
	Glenavon	3	Glentoran	1
Final	**Portadown**	2	Glenavon	1

NATIONAL TEAM 90-91

12/09/90	Yugoslavia (ECQ)	H	Belfast	0-2	
17/10/90	Denmark (ECQ)	H	Belfast	1-1	Clarke
14/11/90	Austria (ECQ)	A	Vienna	0-0	
06/02/91	Poland	H	Belfast	3-1	Taggart 2, Magilton (pen)
27/03/91	Yugoslavia (ECQ)	A	Belgrade	1-4	Hill
01/05/91	Faeroe Isles (ECQ)	H	Belfast	1-1	Clarke

TOP GOALSCORERS

22	McBride	(Glenavon)
20	Hunter	(Crusaders)
19	Hamilton	(Distillery)
	Cowan	(Portadown)
18	McCartney	(Glentoran)

EUROPEAN CUPS

Champions' Cup
PORTADOWN
1st round   FC Porto (Portugal)
A 0-5, H 1-8, (agg. 1-13)

Cup-winners' Cup
GLENTORAN
1st round   Steaua Bucharest
(Romania)
H 1-1, A 0-5, (agg. 1-6)

UEFA Cup
GLENAVON
1st round   Bordeaux (France)
H 0-0, A 0-2, (agg. 0-2)

1990/91 Qualifiers
Champions' Cup   Portadown
Cup-winners' Cup Glenavon
UEFA Cup   Bangor

CHAMPIONSHIP TABLE 90

		Pd	W	D	L	F	A	Pt	GD
1	ROSENBORG	22	13	5	4	60	24	44	+36
2	TROMSO	22	12	6	4	36	21	42	+15
3	MOLDE	22	12	4	6	34	29	40	+5
4	BRANN	22	11	6	5	34	25	39	+9
5	VIKING	22	10	5	7	41	30	35	+11
6	START	22	9	4	9	39	34	31	+5
7	FYLLINGEN	22	7	7	8	23	30	28	-7
8	KONGSVINGER	22	7	6	9	24	32	27	-8
9	STROMSGODSET	22	8	3	11	29	45	27	-16
10	LILLESTROM	22	7	4	11	30	30	25	=
11	VALERENGEN	22	4	4	14	26	53	16	-27
12	MOSS	22	3	4	15	24	47	13	-23

N.B. 3 points for a win

Relegated - VALERENGEN, MOSS
Promoted - SOGNDAL, LYN

DOMESTIC CUP 90

Quarter-Finals	Brann	4	Lillestrom	2
	Kongsvinger	3	Sogndal	2
	Start	0	Fyllingen	1
	Tromso	0	Rosenborg	1
Semi-Finals	Fyllingen	2	Brann	0
	Rosenborg	1	Kongsvinger	0
Final	Rosenborg	5	Fyllingen	1

TOP GOALSCORERS

20	Dahlum	(Start)
17	Jakobsen	(Rosenborg)
13	McCabe	(Tromso)
12	Belsvik	(Molde)
	Storskogen	(Stromsgodset)

EUROPEAN CUPS

Champions' Cup
LILLESTROM
1st round   Club Bruges (Belgium)
H 1-1, A 0-2, (agg. 1-3)

Cup-winners' Cup
VIKING
1st round   FC Liege (Belgium)
H 0-2, A 0-3, (agg. 0-5)

UEFA Cup
ROSENBORG
1st round   Chernomorets Odessa
(USSR)
A 1-3, H 2-1, (agg. 3-4)

1990/91 Qualifiers
Champions' Cup   Rosenborg
Cup-winners' Cup   Fyllingen
UEFA Cup   Tromso

NATIONAL TEAM RESULTS 90-91

22/08/90	Sweden	H	Stavanger	1-2	Ahlsen (pen)
12/09/90	USSR (ECQ)	A	Moscow	0-2	
10/10/90	Hungary (ECQ)	H	Bergen	0-0	
31/10/90	Cameroon	H	Oslo	6-1	Bratseth, Bohinen, Dahlum, Fjortoft 2, Sorloth
07/11/90	Tunisia	A	Tunis	3-1	Dahlum 2, Ingebrigtsen
14/11/90	Cyprus (ECQ)	A	Nicosia	3-0	Sorloth, Bohinen, Brandhaug
17/04/91	Austria	A	Vienna	0-0	
01/05/91	Cyprus (ECQ)	H	Oslo	3-0	Lydersen (pen), Dahlum, Sorloth
23/05/91	Romania	H	Oslo	1-0	Fjortoft
05/06/91	Italy (ECQ)	H	Oslo	2-1	Dahlum, Bohinen

CHAMPIONSHIP TABLE 90-91

		Pd	W	D	L	F	A	Pt	GD
1	ZAGLEBIE LUBIN	30	18	8	4	49	25	44	+24
2	GORNIK ZABRZE	30	15	10	5	55	24	40	+31
3	WISLA KRAKOW	30	13	14	3	52	26	40	+26
4	GKS KATOWICE	30	16	7	7	33	26	39	+7
5	HUTNIK KRAKOW	30	14	9	7	53	34	37	+19
6	LECH POZNAN	30	10	13	7	48	28	33	+20
7	SLASK WROCLAW	30	12	9	9	41	37	33	+4
8	OLIMPIA POZNAN	30	9	12	9	37	41	30	-4
9	LEGIA WARSAW	30	8	12	10	24	24	28	=
10	MOTOR LUBLIN	30	10	8	12	33	38	28	-5
11	LKS LODZ	30	11	6	13	25	36	28	-11
12	PEGROTOUR DEBICA	30	7	12	11	29	44	26	-15
13	RUCH CHORZOW	30	7	11	12	25	35	25	-10
14	ZAWISZA BYDGOSZ.	30	8	7	15	27	41	23	-14
15	STAL MIELEC	30	3	10	17	25	49	16	-24
16	ZAGLEBIE SOSNOW.	30	2	6	22	21	69	10	-48

Relegated - none
Promoted - STAL STALOWA WOLA, WIDZEW LODZ

DOMESTIC CUP 90-91

Quarters Legia Warsaw v LKS Lodz 2-0 0-2 (agg. 2-2; 6-5 on pens.)

Gornik Zabrze v **GKS Katowice** 1-0 0-2 (agg. 1-2)

O. Poznan v Stal Rzeszow 2-1 0-0 (agg. 2-1)

Z. Bydgoszcz v Widzew Lodz 0-1 1-0 (agg. 1-1; 3-1 on pens.)

Semis **GKS Katowice** v Z. Bydgoszcz 3-1 1-0 (agg. 4-1)

O. Poznan v **Legia Warsaw** 0-3 0-1 (agg. 0-4)

Final **GKS Katowice** 1 Legia Warsaw 0

EUROPEAN CUPS

Champions' Cup
LECH POZNAN
1st round	Panathinaikos (Greece)
	H 3-0, A 2-1, (agg. 5-1)
2nd round	Marseille (France)
	H 3-2, A 1-6, (agg. 4-8)

Cup-winners' Cup
LEGIA WARSAW
1st round	Swift Hesperange (Luxembourg)
	H 3-0, A 3-0, (agg. 6-0)
2nd round	Aberdeen (Scotland)
	A 0-0, H 1-0, (agg. 1-0)
Quarter	Sampdoria (Italy)
	H 1-0, A 2-2, (agg. 3-2)
Semi	Manchester United (England)
	H 1-3, A 1-1, (agg. 2-4)

UEFA Cup
ZAGLEBIE LUBIN
| 1st round | Bologna (Italy) |
| | H 0-1, A 0-1, (agg. 0-2) |

GKS KATOWICE
1st round	TPS (Finland)
	H 3-0, A 1-0, (agg. 4-0)
2nd round	Bayer Leverkusen (West Germany)
	H 1-2, A 0-4, (agg. 1-6)

1991/92 Qualifiers
Champions' Cup	Zaglebie Lubin
Cup-winners' Cup	GKS Katowice
UEFA Cup	Gornik Zabrze

NATIONAL TEAM RESULTS 90-91

15/08/90	France	A	Paris	0-0
26/09/90	Romania	A	Bucharest	1-2 Warzycha R.
10/10/90	United States	H	Warsaw	2-3 Kosecki, Ziober
17/10/90	England (ECQ)	A	Wembley	0-2
14/11/90	Turkey (ECQ)	A	Istanbul	1-0 Dziekanowski
18/12/90	Greece	A	Volos	2-1 Soczynski, Kosecki
06/02/91	Northern Ireland	A	Belfast	1-3 Warzycha R.
13/03/91	Finland	H	Warsaw	1-1 Lesiak
27/03/91	Czechoslovakia	A	Olomouc	0-4
17/04/91	Turkey (ECQ)	H	Warsaw	3-0 Tarasiewicz, Urban, Kosecki
01/05/91	Rep. Ireland (ECQ)	A	Dublin	0-0
29/05/91	Wales	H	Radom	0-0

TOP SCORERS

21 Dziubinski (Wisla Krakow)
18 Waligora (H. Krakow)
16 Kraus (G. Zabrze)
15 Cyron (G. Zabrze)
14 Mielcarski (O. Poznan)

PORTUGAL

CHAMPIONSHIP TABLE 90-91

		PD	W	D	L	F	A	Pt	GD
1	BENFICA	38	32	5	1	89	18	69	+71
2	FC PORTO	38	31	5	2	77	22	67	+55
3	SPORTING	38	24	8	6	58	23	56	+35
4	BOAVISTA	38	15	11	12	53	46	41	+7
5	SALGUEIROS	38	12	12	14	32	48	36	-16
6	BEIRA MAR	38	12	12	14	40	49	36	-9
7	BRAGA	38	13	8	17	42	45	34	-3
8	CHAVES	38	10	14	14	49	52	34	-3
9	VIT. GUIMARAES	38	12	10	16	31	40	34	-9
10	MARITIMO	38	12	10	16	37	48	34	-11
11	FARENSE	38	14	6	18	46	47	34	-1
12	GIL VICENTE	38	11	11	16	34	46	33	-12
13	UNIAO	38	9	15	14	30	51	33	-21
14	PENAFIEL	38	12	9	17	34	51	33	-17
15	FAMALICAO	38	11	11	16	33	41	33	-8
16	TIRSENSE	38	10	13	15	39	50	33	-11
17	VIT. SETUBAL	38	11	10	17	53	53	32	=
18	ESTRELA AMADORA	38	9	14	15	37	46	32	-9
19	BELENENSES	38	10	9	19	27	38	29	-11
20	NACIONAL	38	8	11	19	33	60	27	-27

Relegated - TIRSENSE, VITORIA SETUBAL, ESTRELA
AMADORA, BELENENSES, NACIONAL
Promoted - PACOS FERREIRA, ESTORIL, TORRIENSE

TOP GOALSCORERS

25	Rui Aguas	(Benfica)
24	Domingos	(FC Porto)
22	Gomes	(Sporting)
15	Ricky	(Estrela Amadora)

DOMESTIC CUP

Quarter-Finals

Beira Mar	3	Ovarense	0
Feirense	1	Tirsense	0
Boavista	1	Braga	0
FC Porto	2	Benfica	1

Semi-Finals

Beira Mar	2	Boavista	0
Feirense	1	FC Porto	1
(replay)			
FC Porto	2	Feirense	0

Final

FC Porto	3	Beira Mar	1 (a.e.t.)

NATIONAL TEAM RESULTS 90-91

29/08/90	West Germany	H	Lisbon	1-1	Rui Aguas
12/09/90	Finland (ECQ)	A	Helsinki	0-0	
17/10/90	Holland (ECQ)	H	Oporto	1-0	Rui Aguas
20/12/90	United States	H	Oporto	1-0	Domingos
16/01/91	Spain	A	Castellon	1-1	Oceano
23/01/91	Greece (ECQ)	A	Athens	2-3	Rui Aguas, Futre
09/02/91	Malta (ECQ)	A	Ta' Qali	1-0	Futre
20/02/91	Malta (ECQ)	H	Oporto	5-0	Rui Aguas, Leal, Vitor Paneira (pen), Scerri (og), Cadete

GERMANY (West) NATIONAL TEAM RESULTS 90-91

29/08/90	Portugal	A	Lisbon	1-1	Matthaus
10/10/90	Sweden	A	Solna	3-1	Klinsmann, Voller, Brehme
31/10/90	Luxembourg (ECQ)	A	Luxembourg	3-2	Klinsmann, Bein, Voller
19/12/90	Switzerland	H	Stuttgart	4-0	Voller, Riedle, Thom, Matthaus
27/03/91	USSR	H	Frankfurt	2-1	Reuter, Matthaus
01/05/91	Belgium (ECQ)	H	Hanover	1-0	Matthaus
05/06/91	Wales (ECQ)	A	Cardiff	0-1	

EUROPEAN CUPS

Champions' CuP
FC PORTO

1st round	Portadown (Northern Ireland)	H 5-0, A 8-1, (agg. 13-1)
2nd round	Dinamo Bucharest (Romania)	A 0-0, H 4-0, (agg. 4-0)
Quarter	Bayern Munich (West Germany)	A 1-1, H 0-2, (agg. 1-3)

Cup-winners' Cup
ESTRELA AMADORA

1st round	Neuchatel Xamax (Switzerland)	H 1-1, A 1-1, (agg. 2-2; 4-3 on pens.)
2nd round	FC Liege (Belgium)	A 0-2, H 1-0, (agg. 1-2)

UEFA Cup
BENFICA

1st round	Roma (Italy)	A 0-1, H 0-1, (agg. 0-2)

SPORTING

1st round	Mechelen (Belgium)	H 1-0, A 2-2, (agg. 3-2)
2nd round	Politehnica Timisoara (Romania)	H 7-0, A 0-2, (agg. 7-2)
3rd round	Vitesse (Holland)	A 2-0, H 2-1, (agg. 4-1)
Quarter	Bologna (Italy)	A 1-1, H 2-0, (agg. 3-1)
Semi	Internazionale (Italy)	H 0-0, A 0-2, (agg. 0-2)

VITORIA GUIMARAES

1st round	Fenerbahce (Turkey)	A 0-3, H 2-3, (agg. 2-6)

1991/92 Qualifiers

Champions' Cup	Benfica
Cup-winners' Cup	FC Porto
UEFA Cup	Sporting
	Boavista
	Salgueiros

WALES

EUROPEAN CUPS

Cup-winners' Cup
WREXHAM

1st round	Lyngby (Denmark)	H 0-0, A 1-0, (agg. 1-0)
2nd round	Manchester United (England)	A 0-3, H 0-2, (agg. 0-5)

1991/92 Qualifiers
Cup-winners' Cup   Swansea City

DOMESTIC CUP 90-91

Quarters	Stroud	1	**Wrexham**	2
	Colwyn Bay	1	Swansea City	1
(replay)	**Swansea City**	2	Colwyn Bay	0
	Barry Town	1	Abergavenny	1
(replay)	Abergavenny	0	**Barry Town**	1
	Hereford Utd	1	Bangor	1
(replay)	Bangor	0	**Hereford Utd**	0
			(4-5 on pens.)	
Semis	Barry Town v **Swansea City**			
	2-2 0-1 (agg. 2-3)			
	Hereford United v **Wrexham**			
	1-1 1-2 (agg. 2-3)			
Final	**Swansea City**	2	Wrexham	0

NATIONAL TEAM RESULTS 90-91

11/09/90	Denmark	A	Copenhagen	0-1	
17/10/90	Belgium (ECQ)	H	Cardiff	3-1	Rush, Saunders, Hughes
14/11/90	Luxembourg (ECQ)	A	Luxembourg	1-0	Rush
06/02/91	Rep. Ireland	H	Wrexham	0-3	
27/03/91	Belgium (ECQ)	A	Brussels	1-1	Saunders
01/05/91	Iceland	H	Cardiff	1-0	Bodin (pen)
29/05/91	Poland	A	Radom	0-0	

REPUBLIC OF IRELAND

CHAMPIONSHIP TABLE 90-91

		Pd	W	D	L	F	A	Pt	GD
1	DUNDALK	33	22	8	3	52	17	52	+35
2	CORK CITY	33	19	12	2	45	18	50	+27
3	ST. PATRICK'S	33	17	10	6	46	21	44	+25
4	SHELBOURNE	33	18	6	9	59	30	42	+29
5	SLIGO ROVERS	33	13	12	8	34	22	38	+12
6	SHAMROCK ROVERS	33	14	9	10	51	37	37	+14
7	DERRY CITY	33	13	9	11	51	28	35	+23
8	GALWAY UNITED	33	9	5	19	34	61	23	-27
9	BOHEMIANS	33	7	8	18	27	42	22	-15
10	ATHLONE TOWN	33	6	7	20	22	53	19	-31
11	WATERFORD UTD	33	6	5	22	22	62	17	-40
12	LIMERICK CITY	33	6	5	22	21	73	17	-52

Relegated - WATERFORD UNITED, LIMERICK CITY
Promoted - DROGHEDA UNITED, BRAY WANDERERS

DOMESTIC CUP 90-91

Quarter-finals	Athlone Town	0	Shamrock Rovers	0
(replay)	**Shamrock Rovers**	1	Athlone Town	0
	Limerick City	1	**Galway United**	2
	Kilkenny City	1	Ashtown Villa	0
	Waterford United	0	**St. James' Gate**	1
Semi-finals	Kilkenny City	0	**Shamrock Rovers**	1
	St. James' Gate	1	**Galway United**	3
Final	**Galway United**	1	Shamrock Rovers	0

TOP GOALSCORERS

18	Hanrahan	(Dundalk)
15	Morley	(St. Patrick's Athletic)
14	Arkins	(Shamrock Rovers)
	Newe	(Shelbourne)
12	Ennis	(St. Patrick's Athletic)
	Fenlon	(St. Patrick's Athletic)

EUROPEAN CUPS

Champions' Cup
ST. PATRICK'S ATHLETIC
1st round   Dinamo Bucharest
(Romania)
A 0-4, H 1-1, (agg. 1-5)

Cup-winners' Cup
BRAY WANDERERS
Prelim.   Trabzonspor (Turkey)
H 1-1, A 0-2, (agg. 1-3)

UEFA Cup
DERRY CITY
1st round   Vitesse (Holland)
H 0-1, A 0-0, (agg. 0-1)

1991/92 Qualifiers
Champions' Cup   Dundalk
Cup-winners' Cup   Galway United
UEFA Cup   Cork City

NATIONAL TEAM RESULTS 90-91

12/09/90	Morocco	H	Dublin	1-0	Kelly D.
17/10/90	Turkey (ECQ)	H	Dublin	5-0	Aldridge 3 (1 pen), O'Leary, Quinn
14/11/90	England (ECQ)	H	Dublin	1-1	Cascarino
06/02/91	Wales	A	Wrexham	3-0	Quinn 2, Byrne
27/03/91	England (ECQ)	A	Wembley	1-1	Quinn
01/05/91	Poland (ECQ)	H	Dublin	0-0	
22/05/91	Chile	H	Dublin	1-1	Kelly D.
01/06/91	United States	A	Foxboro	1-1	Cascarino

CHAMPIONSHIP TABLE 90-91

		Pd	W	D	L	F	A	Pt	GD
1	UNI. CRAIOVA	34	22	6	6	74	26	50	+48
2	STEAUA BUCHAREST	34	20	10	4	67	28	50	+39
3	DINAMO BUCHAREST	34	16	11	7	54	27	43	+27
4	INTER SIBIU	34	18	2	14	56	46	38	+10
5	GLORIA BISTRITA	34	15	7	12	51	38	37	+13
6	POLI. TIMISOARA	34	14	7	13	45	45	35	=
7	PETROLUL PL'ESTI	34	15	5	14	48	49	35	-1
8	ARGES PITESTI	34	13	8	13	49	42	34	+7
9	FCM BRASOV	34	14	6	14	47	45	34	+2
10	FARUL CONSTANTA	34	12	10	12	40	40	34	=
11	RAPID BUCHAREST	34	13	6	15	44	45	32	-1
12	SPORTUL STUD.	34	10	12	12	45	53	32	-8
13	PROGRESUL BRAILA	34	13	5	16	33	49	31	-16
14	CORVINUL H'DOARA	34	15	2	17	47	62	30	-15
15	FC BACAU	34	11	7	16	32	42	29	-10
16	JIUL PETROSANI	34	11	6	17	46	65	28	-19
17	BIHOR ORADEA	34	7	8	19	40	75	18	-35
18	UNI. CLUJ-NAPOCA	34	5	6	23	26	67	16	-41

N.B. CORVINUL HUNEDOARA 2 pts deducted; BIHOR ORADEA 4 pts deducted.

Relegated - JIUL PETROSANI, BIHOR ORADEA, UNIVERSITATEA CLUJ-NAPOCA

Promoted - ASA TIRGU MURES, OTELUL GALATI, ELECTROPUTERE CRAIOVA

DOMESTIC CUP 90-91

Quarters	D. Bucharest v **U. Craiova**	1-0	0-2	(agg. 1-2)
	S. Bucharest v **U. Alba Iulia**	0-3	2-1	(agg. 2-4)
	Farul Constanta v **In. Sibiu**	2-1	0-1	(agg. 2-2; Inter Sibiu on away goals)
	Arges Pitesti v **FC Bacau**	2-1	0-2	(agg. 2-3)
Semis	**Uni. Craiova** v U. Alba Iulia	4-0	0-3	(agg. 4-3)
	Inter Sibiu v **FC Bacau**	0-0	0-1	(agg. 0-1)
Final	**Universitatea Craiova** 2		FC Bacau 1	

EUROPEAN CUPS

Champions' Cup
DINAMO BUCHAREST

1st round	St. Patrick's Athletic (Republic of Ireland) H 4-0, A 1-1, (agg. 5-1)
2nd round	FC Porto (Portugal) H 0-0, A 0-4, (agg. 0-4)

Cup-winners' Cup
STEAUA BUCHAREST

1st round	Glentoran (Northern Ireland) A 1-1, H 5-0, (agg. 6-1)
2nd round	Montpellier (France) A 0-5, H 0-3, (agg. 0-8)

UEFA Cup
PETROLUL PLOIESTI

1st round	Anderlecht (Belgium) A 0-2, H 0-2, (agg. 0-4)

UNIVERSITATEA CRAIOVA

1st round	Partizani Tirana (Albania) A 1-0, H 1-0, (agg. 2-0)
2nd round	Borussia Dortmund (West Germany) H 0-3, A 0-1, (agg. 0-4)

POLITEHNICA TIMISOARA

1st round	Atletico Madrid (Spain) H 2-0, A 0-1, (agg. 2-1)
2nd round	Sporting (Portugal) A 0-7, H 2-0, (agg. 2-7)

1991/92 Qualifiers

Champions' Cup	Univ. Craiova
Cup-winners' Cup	FC Bacau
UEFA Cup	Steaua Bucharest
	Dinamo Bucharest

NATIONAL TEAM RESULTS 90-91

29/08/90	USSR	A	Moscow	2-1	Lacatus (pen), Lupescu
12/09/90	Scotland (ECQ)	A	Glasgow	1-2	Camataru
26/09/90	Poland	H	Bucharest	2-1	Lazar, Rotariu
17/10/90	Bulgaria (ECQ)	H	Bucharest	0-3	
05/12/90	San Marino (ECQ)	H	Bucharest	6-0	Sabau, Mateut, Raducioiu, Lupescu, Badea, Petrescu
27/03/91	San Marino (ECQ)	A	Serravalle	3-1	Hagi (pen), Raducioiu, Timofte D.
03/04/91	Switzerland (ECQ)	A	Neuchatel	0-0	
17/04/91	Spain	A	Caceres	2-0	Timofte I., Balint
23/05/91	Norway	A	Oslo	0-1	

TOP SCORERS

24 Hanganu
(Corvinul Hunedoara)

17 Bicu
(Jiul Petrosani)

15 Damaschin
(Din. Bucharest)
Gerstenmajer
(FCM Brasov)

SCOTLAND

CHAMPIONSHIP TABLE 90-91

		Pd	W	D	L	F	A	Pt	GD
1	RANGERS	36	24	7	5	62	23	55	+39
2	ABERDEEN	36	22	9	5	62	27	53	+35
3	CELTIC	36	17	7	12	52	38	41	+14
4	DUNDEE UNITED	36	17	7	12	41	29	41	+12
5	HEARTS	36	14	7	15	48	55	35	-7
6	MOTHERWELL	36	12	9	15	51	50	33	+1
7	ST. JOHNSTONE	36	11	9	16	41	54	31	-13
8	DUNFERMLINE	36	8	11	17	38	61	27	-23
9	HIBERNIAN	36	6	13	17	24	51	25	-27
10	ST. MIRREN	36	5	9	22	28	59	19	-31

Relegated - none
Promoted - FALKIRK, AIRDRIEONIANS

DOMESTIC CUP 90-91

Quarter-Finals	Celtic	2	Rangers	0	
	Motherwell	0	Morton	0	
(replay)	Morton	1	**Motherwell**	1	
			(4-5 on pens.)		
	St. Johnstone	5	Ayr United	2	
	Dundee United	3	Dundee	1	
Semi-Finals	Motherwell	0	Celtic	0	
(replay)	Celtic	2	**Motherwell**	4	
	Dundee United	2	St. Johnstone	1	
Final	**Motherwell**	4	Dundee United	3	
			(a.e.t.)		

NATIONAL TEAM 90-91

12/09/90	Romania (ECQ)	H	Glasgow	2-1	Robertson, McCoist
17/10/90	Switzerland (ECQ)	H	Glasgow	2-1	Robertson (pen), McAllister
14/11/90	Bulgaria (ECQ)	A	Sofia	1-1	McCoist
06/02/91	USSR	H	Glasgow	0-1	
27/03/91	Bulgaria (ECQ)	H	Glasgow	1-1	Collins
01/05/91	San Marino (ECQ)	A	Serravalle	2-0	Strachan (pen), Durie

TOP GOALSCORERS

18	Coyne (Celtic)
14	Arnott (Motherwell)
	Gillhaus (Aberdeen)
13	Jess (Aberdeen)
12	Jackson (Dundee United)
	Robertson (Hearts)
	Walters (Rangers)

EUROPEAN CUPS

Champions' Cup
RANGERS

1st round	Valletta (Malta)
	A 4-0, H 6-0, (agg. 10-0)
2nd round	Red Star Belgrade (Yugoslavia)
	A 0-3, H 1-1, (agg. 1-4)

Cup-winners' Cup
ABERDEEN

1st round	NEA Salamis (Cyprus)
	A 2-0, H 3-0, (agg. 5-0)
2nd round	Legia Warsaw (Poland)
	H 0-0, A 0-1, (agg. 0-1)

UEFA Cup
DUNDEE UNITED

1st round	FH (Iceland)
	A 3-1, H 2-2, (agg. 5-3)
2nd round	Vitesse (Holland)
	A 0-1, H 0-4, (agg. 0-5)

HEARTS

1st round	Dnepropetrovsk (USSR)
	A 1-1, H 3-1, (agg. 4-2)
2nd round	Bologna (Italy)
	H 3-1, A 0-3, (agg. 3-4)

1990/91 Qualifiers

Champions' Cup	Rangers
Cup-winners' Cup	Motherwell
UEFA Cup	Aberdeen
	Celtic

CHAMPIONSHIP TABLE 90

		Pd	W	D	L	F	A	Pt	GD
1	DINAMO KIEV	24	14	6	4	44	20	34	+24
2	CSKA MOSCOW	24	13	5	6	43	26	31	+17
3	DINAMO MOSCOW	24	12	7	5	27	24	31	+3
4	TORPEDO MOSCOW	24	13	4	7	28	24	30	+4
5	SPARTAK MOSCOW	24	12	5	7	39	26	29	+13
6	DNEPROPETROVSK	24	11	6	7	39	26	28	+13
7	ARARAT EREVAN	24	8	7	9	25	23	23	+2
8	SHAKTYOR DONETSK	24	6	10	8	23	31	22	-8
9	CHERNOMORETS	24	8	3	13	23	29	19	-6
10	PAMIR DUSHANBE	24	7	4	13	26	34	18	-8
11	METALIST KHARKOV	24	5	8	11	13	28	18	-15
12	DINAMO MINSK	24	6	3	15	20	34	15	-14
13	ROTOR VOLGOGRAD	24	4	6	14	14	39	14	-25

Relegated - ROTOR VOLGOGRAD
Promoted - SPARTAK VLADIKAVKAZ, PAKHTAKOR
TASHKENT, METALLURG ZAPOROZHJE,
LOKOMOTIV MOSCOW

1991/92 Euro Qualifiers

Champions' Cup	Dinamo Kiev
Cup-winners' Cup	CSKA Moscow
UEFA Cup	Dinamo Moscow
	Torpedo Moscow
	Spartak Moscow

TOP GOALSCORERS

12	Protasov	(Dinamo Kiev)
	Shmarov	(Spartak Moscow)
10	Son	(Dnepropetrovsk)

DOMESTIC CUP

Quarter-Finals

Spartak Moscow	0
Torpedo Moscow	0
(1-3 on pens.)	
Ararat Erevan	1
Chernomorets	0
CSKA Moscow	4
Dinamo Minsk	1
Lok. Moscow	2
Sverdlovsk	0

Semi-Finals

CSKA Moscow	3
Lokomotiv Moscow	0
Torpedo Moscow	0
Ararat Erevan	0
(5-4 on pens.)	

Final

CSKA Moscow	3
Torpedo Moscow	2

NATIONAL TEAM RESULTS 90-91

29/08/90	Romania	H	Moscow	1-2	Mikhailichenko
12/09/90	Norway (ECQ)	H	Moscow	2-0	Kanchelskis, Kuznetsov O.
09/10/90	Israel	H	Moscow	3-0	Yuran 2, Litovchenko
03/11/90	Italy (ECQ)	A	Rome	0-0	
21/11/90	United States	N	Port of Spain	0-0	
24/11/90	Trinidad & Tobago	A	Port of Spain	2-0	Shalimov, Tseiba
30/11/90	Guatemala	A	Guatemala	3-0	Mostovoj, Dobrovolsky, Kolyvanov
06/02/91	Scotland	A	Glasgow	1-0	Kuznetsov D.
27/03/91	Germany	A	Frankfurt	1-2	Dobrovolsky (pen)
17/04/91	Hungary (ECQ)	A	Budapest	1-0	Mikhailichenko
21/05/91	England	A	Wembley	1-3	Wright (og)
23/05/91	Argentina	N	Manchester	1-1	Kolyvanov
29/05/91	Cyprus (ECQ)	H	Moscow	4-0	Mostovoj, Mikhailichenko, Korneev, Aleinikov
13/06/91	Sweden	A	Gothenburg	3-2	Yuran, Kuznetsov D., Korneev
16/06/91	Italy	N	Solna	1-1	Korneev

SOVIET UNION

EUROPEAN CUPS

Champions' Cup
SPARTAK MOSCOW

1st round	Sparta Prague (Czechoslovakia)	A 2-0, H 2-0, (agg. 4-0)
2nd round	Napoli (Italy)	A 0-0, H 0-0, (agg. 0-0; 5-3 on pens.)
Quarter	Real Madrid (Spain)	H 0-0, A 3-1, (agg. 3-1)
Semi-Final	Marseille (France)	H 1-3, A 1-2, (agg. 2-5)

Cup-winners' Cup
DINAMO KIEV

1st round	KuPS (Finland)	A 2-2, H 4-0, (agg. 6-2)
2nd round	Dukla Prague (Czechoslovakia)	H 1-0, A 2-2, (agg. 3-2)
Quarter	Barcelona (Spain)	H 2-3, A 1-1, (agg. 3-4)

UEFA Cup
DNEPROPETROVSK

1st round	Hearts (Scotland)	H 1-1, A 1-3, (agg. 2-4)

TORPEDO MOSCOW

1st round	GAIS (Sweden)	H 4-1, A 1-1, (agg. 5-2)
2nd round	Sevilla (Spain)	H 3-1, A 1-2, (agg. 4-3)
3rd round	Monaco (France)	H 2-1, A 2-1, (agg. 4-2)
Quarter	Brondby (Denmark)	A 0-1, H 1-0, (agg. 1-1; 2-4 on pens.)

CHERNOMORETS ODESSA

1st round	Rosenborg (Norway)	H 3-1, A 1-2, (agg. 4-3)
2nd round	Monaco (France)	H 0-0, A 0-1, (agg. 0-1)

SPAIN

EUROPEAN CUPS

Champions' Cup
REAL MADRID

1st round	OB (Denmark)	A 4-1, H 6-0, (agg. 10-1)
2nd round	FC Swarovski Tirol (Austria)	H 9-1, A 2-2, (agg. 11-3)
Quarter	Spartak Moscow (USSR)	A 0-0, H 1-3, (agg. 1-3)

Cup-winners' Cup
BARCELONA

1st round	Trabzonspor (Turkey)	A 0-1, H 7-2, (agg. 7-3)
2nd round	Fram (Iceland)	A 2-1, H 3-0, (agg. 5-1)
Quarter	Dinamo Kiev (USSR)	A 3-2, H 1-1, (agg. 4-3)
Semi-Final	Juventus (Italy)	H 3-1, A 0-1, (agg. 3-2)
Final	Manchester United (England) 1-2	

UEFA Cup

ATLETICO MADRID

1st round	Politehnica Timisoara (Romania)	A 0-2, H 1-0, (agg. 1-2)

VALENCIA

1st round	Iraklis (Greece)	A 0-0, H 2-0, (agg. 2-0)
2nd round	Roma (Italy)	H 1-1, A 1-2, (agg. 2-3)

SEVILLA

1st round	PAOK (Greece)	H 0-0, A 0-0, (agg. 0-0; 4-3 on pens.)
2nd round	Torpedo Moscow (USSR)	A 1-3, H 2-1, (agg. 3-4)

REAL SOCIEDAD

1st round	Lausanne (Switzerland)	A 2-3, H 1-0, (agg. 3-3; won on away goals)
2nd round	Partizan Belgrade (Yugoslavia)	H 1-0, A 0-1, (agg. 1-1; 3-4 on pens.)

CHAMPIONSHIP TABLE 90-91

		Pd	W	D	L	F	A	Pt	GD
1	BARCELONA	38	25	7	6	74	33	57	+41
2	ATLETICO MADRID	38	17	13	8	52	28	47	+24
3	REAL MADRID	38	20	6	12	63	37	46	+26
4	OSASUNA	38	15	15	8	43	34	45	+9
5	SPORTING GIJON	38	16	12	10	50	37	44	+13
6	OVIEDO	38	13	16	9	36	35	42	+1
7	VALENCIA	38	15	10	13	44	40	40	+4
8	SEVILLA	38	15	8	15	45	47	38	-2
9	VALLADOLID	38	12	13	13	38	40	37	-2
10	LOGRONES	38	13	11	14	28	35	37	-7
11	BURGOS	38	10	17	11	32	27	37	+5
12	ATHLETIC BILBAO	38	15	6	17	41	50	36	-9
13	REAL SOCIEDAD	38	11	14	13	39	45	36	-6
14	TENERIFE	38	14	7	17	37	53	35	-16
15	MALLORCA	38	9	16	13	32	40	34	-8
16	ESPANOL	38	12	10	16	39	47	34	-8
17	ZARAGOZA	38	11	11	16	36	40	33	-4
18	CADIZ	38	7	15	16	29	41	29	-12
19	CASTELLON	38	8	12	18	27	48	28	-21
20	BETIS	38	6	13	19	37	65	25	-28

Relegated - CASTELLON, BETIS

Promoted - ALBACETE, DEPORTIVO LA CORUNA

1991/92 European Cups Qualifiers

Champions' Cup	Barcelona
Cup-winners' Cup	Atletico Madrid
UEFA Cup	Real Madrid, Osasuna, Sporting Gijon, Oviedo

TOP GOALSCORERS

19	Butragueno	(Real Madrid)
17	Aldridge	(Real Sociedad)
16	Manolo	(Atletico Madrid)
	Luhovy	(Sporting Gijon)
15	Luis Enrique	(Sporting Gijon)

DOMESTIC CUP

Quarter-Finals

Sevilla v **Barcelona**
0-4   0-3   (agg. 0-7)

Valencia v **Mallorca**
1-0   1-3   (agg. 2-3)

Logrones v **Sporting Gijon**
2-0   0-3   (agg. 2-3)

Valladolid v **Atletico Madrid**
0-2   1-0   (agg. 1-2)

Semi-Finals

Sporting Gijon v **Mallorca**
0-1   0-1   (agg. 0-2)

Barcelona v **Atletico Madrid**
0-2   3-2   (agg. 3-4)

Final

Atletico Madrid 1 Mallorca 0
(a.e.t.)

NATIONAL TEAM RESULTS 90-91

12/09/90	Brazil	H	Gijon	3-0	Carlos, Fernando, Michel
10/10/90	Iceland (ECQ)	H	Seville	2-1	Butragueno, Carlos
14/11/90	Czechoslovakia (ECQ)	A	Prague	2-3	Roberto, Carlos
19/12/90	Albania (ECQ)	H	Seville	9-0	Amor, Carlos 2, Butragueno 4,Hierro, Bakero
16/01/91	Portugal	H	Castellon	1-1	Moya
20/02/91	France (ECQ)	A	Paris	1-3	Bakero
27/03/91	Hungary	H	Santander	2-4	Manolo (pen), Carlos
17/04/91	Romania	H	Caceres	0-2	

SWEDEN

CHAMPIONSHIP TABLE 90

		Pd	W	D	L	F	A	Pd	GD
1	IFK GOTHENBURG	22	14	3	5	39	22	45	+17
2	IFK NORRKOPING	22	12	4	6	41	23	40	+18
3	OREBRO	22	10	6	6	23	17	36	+6
4	OSTER	22	10	6	6	28	27	36	+1
5	DJURGARDEN	22	9	6	7	37	23	33	+14
6	MALMO	22	6	10	6	20	15	28	+5
7	GAIS	22	7	7	8	17	17	28	=
8	AIK	22	8	3	11	25	39	27	-14
9	HALMSTAD	22	7	5	10	27	34	26	-7
10	BRAGE	22	5	9	8	23	26	24	-3
11	ORGYRYTE	22	6	3	13	22	40	21	-18
12	HAMMARBY	22	5	4	13	32	51	19	-19

CHAMPIONSHIP PLAY-OFFS
Semi-finals   IFK Gothenburg bt Orebro
IFK Norrkoping bt Oster
Final   IFK Gothenburg bt IFK Norrkoping
(IFK Gothenburg Champions)

Relegated - BRAGE, ORGRYTE, HAMMARBY
Promoted - GIF SUNDSVALL

DOMESTIC CUP 90-91

Quarter-Finals	Helsingborg	3	BK Forward	0
	Oster	3	IFK Eskilstuna	1
	IFK Norrkoping	2	Gefle	0
	BP	0	Malmo	0
	(4-3 on pens.)			
Semi-Finals	BP	0	Oster	3
	IFK Norrkoping	3	Helsingborg	0
Final	IFK Norrkoping	4	Oster	1

TOP GOALSCORERS

10	Eskelinen	(IFK Gothenburg)
8	Andersson P.	(IFK Norrkoping)
	Hellstrom	(IFK Norrkoping)
	Andersson K.	(IFK Gothenburg)
	Karlstrom	(Djurgarden)
	Skoog	(Djurgarden)
	Jonsson	(Hammarby)

EUROPEAN CUPS

Champions' Cup
MALMO
1st round   Besiktas (Turkey)
H 3-2, A 2-2, (agg. 5-4)
2nd round Dynamo Dresden
(East Germany)
A 1-1, H 1-1, (agg. 2-2;
4-5 on pens.)

Cup-winners' Cup
DJURGARDEN
1st round   Fram (Iceland)
A 0-3, H 1-1, (agg. 1-4)

UEFA Cup
IFK NORRKOPING
1st round   Cologne (W. Germany)
H 0-0, A 1-3, (agg. 1-3)

GAIS
1st round   Torp. Moscow (USSR)
A 1-4, H 1-1, (agg. 2-5)

1991/92 Qualifiers
Champions' Cup   IFK Gothenburg
Cup-winners' Cup IFK Norrkoping
UEFA Cup   Orebro, Oster

NATIONAL TEAM RESULTS 90-91

22/08/90	Norway	A	Stavanger	2-1	Engqvist, Fjellstrom
05/09/90	Denmark	H	Vasteras	0-1	
26/09/90	Bulgaria	H	Solna	2-0	Corneliusson, Andersson K.
10/10/90	West Germany	H	Solna	1-3	Rehn (pen)
17/04/91	Greece	A	Athens	2-2	Erlingmark, Mild
01/05/91	Austria	H	Solna	6-0	Andersson K. 3, Rehn, Dahlin 2
05/06/91	Colombia	H	Solna	2-2	Brolin, Andersson K.
13/06/91	USSR	H	Gothenburg	2-3	Brolin 2
15/06/91	Denmark	H	Norrkoping	4-0	Dahlin 2, Andersson K. (pen), Brolin

CHAMPIONSHIP TABLE

		Pd	W	D	L	F	A	Pt	GD
1	GRASSHOPPERS	36	16	14	6	56	32	33	+24
2	SION	36	13	18	5	45	35	29	+10
3	NEUCHATEL XAMAX	36	13	16	7	41	28	29	+13
4	LAUSANNE	36	14	14	8	54	43	29	+11
5	LUGANO	36	13	13	10	43	37	27	+6
6	YOUNG BOYS	36	9	17	10	56	52	24	+4
7	SERVETTE	36	10	15	11	46	51	23	-5
8	LUZERN	36	11	11	14	46	48	22	-2
9	ST. GALLEN	22	7	8	7	26	26	22	=
10	AARAU	22	3	9	10	19	30	15	-11
11	FC ZURICH	22	3	6	13	21	45	12	-24
12	WETTINGEN	22	3	5	14	24	50	11	-26

N.B. After 22 matches the top eight play off for the title, taking half their points total. Half points are rounded upwards. The bottom four enter two promotion/relegation play-off groups with the top 12 Second Division teams.

Relegated - none   Promoted - none

DOMESTIC CUP 90-91

Quarter-Finals	Tuggen	0	**Chiasso**	4
	Young Boys	2	Grasshoppers	0
	Sion	1	St. Gallen	0
	FC Zurich	4	La-Chaux-de-Fonds	1
Semi-Finals	**Young Boys**	5	FC Zurich	1
	Sion	2	Chiasso	1
Final	Sion	3	Young Boys	2

TOP GOALSCORERS

17	Zuffi	(Young Boys)
16	Eriksen	(Luzern)
15	De Vicente	(Grasshoppers)

EUROPEAN CUPS

Champions' Cup
GRASSHOPPERS
1st round   Red Star Belgrade (Yugoslavia)
             A 1-1, H 1-4, (agg. 2-5)

Cup-winners' Cup
NEUCHATEL XAMAX
1st round   Estrela Amadora (Portugal)
             A 1-1, H 1-1, (agg. 2-2; 3-4 on pens.)

UEFA Cup
LAUSANNE
1st round   Real Sociedad (Spain)
             H 3-2, A 0-1, (agg. 3-3; lost on away goals)

LUZERN
1st round   MTK-VM (Hungary)
             A 1-1, H 2-1, (agg. 3-2)
2nd round   Admira Wacker (Austria)
             H 0-1, A 1-1, (agg. 1-2)

1991/92 Qualifiers
Champions' Cup   Grasshoppers
Cup-winners' Cup   Sion
UEFA Cup   Neuchatel X.
                    Lausanne

NATIONAL TEAM RESULTS 90-91

21/08/90	Austria	A	Vienna	3-1	Turkyilmaz 2, Knup
12/09/90	Bulgaria (ECQ)	H	Geneva	2-0	Hottiger, Bickel
17/10/90	Scotland (ECQ)	A	Glasgow	1-2	Knup (pen)
14/11/90	San Marino (ECQ)	A	Serravalle	4-0	Sutter A., Chapuisat, Knup, Chassot
19/12/90	Germany	A	Stuttgart	0-4	
02/02/91	United States	A	Miami	1-0	Knup
03/02/91	Colombia	N	Miami	3-2	Koller, Sutter B. 2
12/03/91	Liechtenstein	A	Balzers	6-0	Hermann, Knupp 3 (1 pen), Turkyilmaz, Aeby
03/04/91	Romania (ECQ)	H	Neuchatel	0-0	
01/05/91	Bulgaria (ECQ)	A	Sofia	3-2	Knup 2, Turkyilmaz
05/06/91	San Marino (ECQ)	H	St. Gallen	7-0	Knup 2, Hottiger, Sutter B., Hermann, Ohrel, Turkyilmaz

CHAMPIONSHIP TABLE 90-91

		Pd	W	D	L	F	A	Pt	GD
1	BESIKTAS	30	20	9	1	63	24	69	+39
2	GALATASARAY	30	19	7	4	63	31	64	+32
3	TRABZONSPOR	30	14	9	7	55	37	51	+18
4	SARIYER	30	11	12	7	39	34	45	+5
5	FENERBAHCE	30	12	8	10	53	53	44	=
6	BAKIRKOYSPOR	30	12	7	11	53	41	43	+12
7	ANKARAGUCU	30	11	8	11	46	43	41	+3
8	BURSASPOR	30	11	5	14	31	36	38	-5
9	BOLUSPOR	30	8	13	9	35	37	37	-2
10	GENCLERBIRLIGI	30	9	9	12	36	47	36	-11
11	AYDINSPOR	30	7	13	10	44	51	34	-7
12	KONYASPOR	30	10	4	16	33	45	34	-12
13	GAZIANTEPSPOR	30	9	6	15	29	45	33	-16
14	ZEYTINBURNU	30	6	11	13	26	40	29	-14
15	KARSIYAKA	30	6	8	16	32	50	26	-18
16	ADANASPOR	30	5	11	14	34	58	26	-24

Relegated - ZEYTINBURNU, KARSIYAKA, ADANASPOR
Promoted - SAMSUNSPOR, ALTAY, ADANA DEMIRSPOR

DOMESTIC CUP 90-91

Quarters	Galatasaray	2	Besiktas	2	(7-6 on pens.)
	Fenerbahce	2	Sariyer	2	(7-6 on pens.)
	Trabzonspor	2	Bakirkoyspor	1	
	Ankaragucu	4	Aydinspor	0	
Semis	Fenerbahce	1	Ankaragucu	3	
	Galatasaray	2	Trabzonspor	1	
Final	Galatasaray	3	Ankaragucu	1	(a.e.t.)

NATIONAL TEAM 90-91

05/09/90	Hungary	A	Budapest	1-4	Tanju
17/10/90	Rep. Ireland (ECQ)	A	Dublin	0-5	
14/11/90	Poland (ECQ)	H	Istanbul	0-1	
27/02/91	Yugoslavia	H	Izmir	1-1	Ugur
27/03/91	Tunisia	A	Tunis	0-0	
17/04/91	Poland (ECQ)	A	Warsaw	0-3	
01/05/91	England (ECQ)	H	Izmir	0-1	

TOP GOALSCORERS

31	Tanju	(Galatasaray)
16	Sabotic	(Ankaragucu)
	Feyyaz	(Besiktas)

EUROPEAN CUPS

Champions' Cup
BESIKTAS
1st round   Malmo (Sweden)
             A 2-3, H 2-2, (agg. 4-5)

Cup-winners' Cup
TRABZONSPOR
Prelim.   Bray Wanderers
             (Republic of Ireland)
             A 1-1, H 2-0, (agg. 3-1)
1st round   Barcelona (Spain)
             H 1-0, A 2-7, (agg. 3-7)

UEFA Cup
FENERBAHCE
1st round   Vitoria Guimaraes
             (Portugal)
             H 3-0, A 3-2, (agg. 6-2)
2nd round   Atalanta (Italy)
             H 0-1, A 1-4, (agg. 1-5)

1991/92 Qualifiers
Champions' Cup   Besiktas
Cup-winners' Cup Galatasaray
UEFA Cup   Trabzonspor

W A L E S – see page 29